ROBERT O'HARA BURKE
AND THE
AUSTRALIAN EXPLORING
EXPEDITION OF 1860

Published @ 2017 Trieste Publishing Pty Ltd

ISBN 9780649694563

Robert O'Hara Burke and the Australian Exploring Expedition of 1860 by Andrew Jackson

Edited by Trieste Publishing Pty Ltd.
Cover @ 2017

www.triestepublishing.com

ANDREW JACKSON

ROBERT O'HARA BURKE AND THE AUSTRALIAN EXPLORING EXPEDITION OF 1860

 Trieste

ROBERT O'HARA BURKE

AND THE

AUSTRALIAN EXPLORING
EXPEDITION OF 1860.

By ANDREW JACKSON.

ROBERT O'HARA BURKE.

LONDON:
SMITH, ELDER AND CO., 65, CORNHILL.

M.DCCC.LXII.

TO

MISS HESTER ALBINIA BURKE,

WHOSE NAME WAS THE LAST UTTERANCE FROM THE LIPS OF HER

LOVED AND GALLANT BROTHER,

𝕿𝕳𝖎𝖘 𝖁𝖔𝖑𝖚𝖒𝖊,

RECORDING HIS HEROIC ACHIEVEMENT,

IS INSCRIBED, WITH FEELINGS OF SINCERE SYMPATHY,

BY HER FAITHFUL SERVANT,

THE COMPILER.

PREFACE.

SERVING in the same regiment with the head of the
family to which belonged Robert O'Hara Burke, and
sharing the personal attachment which every member
of that family seems to inspire in those who know them,
I naturally felt a deep interest in the noble career
and melancholy fate of the gallant Leader of the Australian Exploring Expedition of 1860. Animated by
a strong feeling of admiration for the active energy,
stedfast courage, and patient endurance shown by
this brave man, in every stage of this arduous enterprise, I undertook the present attempt to record the
incidents of the Exploration of Central Australia so
successfully achieved.

My task has been limited to arranging consecutively the letters and journals of the explorers, and
forming the whole into a connected narrative of the

progress and results of the Expedition, the vicissitudes of the exploring party, and the fatal disasters which overtook them at last. In doing so, I have not been able to refrain from censuring the conduct of one of the party in particular, as well as vindicating Mr. Burke; who, in his character as Leader of the Expedition, presents a noble example of those qualities which are called for in the soldier, the voyager, and the pioneer of civilization.

ANDREW JACKSON,
Ensign, 3rd Buffs.

Malta, June, 1862.

CONTENTS.

APPENDICES.

ROBERT O'HARA BURKE

AND THE

AUSTRALIAN EXPLORING EXPEDITION OF 1860.

CHAPTER I.

INTRODUCTORY.

THE vast extent of the unexplored portion of the great Australian continent had long baffled numerous efforts made to penetrate its mysterious and silent depths. Although it was believed that the immense tract of country lying between the 15th and 30th parallels of south latitude, and 120th and 145th meridians of east longitude, contained, in all probability, habitable space sufficient to afford an eligible home to millions of civilized beings, yet none of the parties equipped at different times to explore it had ever done more than obtain a partial and unsatisfying success. Difficulties caused by want of water, impassability of ground, and dangers connected with

1

the open hostility or treacherous friendship of the aboriginal tribes, had repelled the intrepid efforts of such men as Sturt, Gregory, Oxley, and others, who had vainly striven to overcome them; while the mysterious fate of the esteemed and lamented Leichardt, although it did not prevent fresh attempts from being made, had yet exercised a depressing and melancholy effect on the spirits of the enterprising public, tending, on the whole, to produce a belief that, with regard to certain boundaries of Central Australia, it might be safely said, " Hither shalt thou come, and no farther."

To the Anglo-Saxon temperament, however, difficulties only serve as fresh incentives to exertion. The inhabitants of the colony of Victoria,* urged by a recollection of the generous spirit displayed by neighbouring colonies whose unassisted efforts had effected the more recent discoveries, and stimulated by the feeling that it behoved Victoria, as the wealthiest and most important of the group, to take her share in a work no less of the highest interest and importance in a scientific point of view than likely to prove hereafter of great commercial advantage to themselves, convened a public meeting in Melbourne on the 1st of September, 1858, for the purpose of promoting the great object of Australian exploration. A donation of one thousand pounds, munificently

* Despatch from Governor Sir Henry Barkly to the Duke of Newcastle, dated August 21, 1860.

offered by an anonymous individual through the columns of the *Argus* newspaper, formed the nucleus of a private subscription, which speedily reached the sum of three thousand two hundred pounds, and a further sum of six thousand pounds having been subsequently voted by the Colonial Legislature towards the expenses of the expedition, the whole fund was placed at the disposal of a committee of the Royal Society of Victoria, presided over by Sir Henry Barkly, K.C.B., governor of the colony.

This society, which had already had under its consideration the great assistance likely to be derived from the use of camels in the interior, had previously made arrangements to import from India a number of these animals, twenty-four of which were successfully landed in first-rate order in the early part of 1860. After some further preliminaries and consideration as to the selection of a leader for the expedition, the choice of the committee at length fell on ROBERT O'HARA BURKE, ESQ., one of the superintendents of the police force of the colony, a short account of whose family and previous career will be found in the succeeding chapter.

CHAPTER II.

MR. BURKE'S FAMILY.

JAMES HARDIMAN BURKE, ESQ., representative of one
of the old families in the county of Galway, in
Ireland, was engaged, like his sons after him, in the
service of his country, having been present with the
7th Royal Fusiliers at the capture of the islands
of Martinique and Guadaloupe.   After having
served several years in the army, he retired to the
family estates at St. Clerans, and died in January,
1854.

His eldest, and now only surviving son, John
Hardiman Burke, served seventeen years in the
88th Foot, with whom he was employed in the
Mediterranean, West Indies, Nova Scotia, and other
foreign stations.   He accompanied his regiment to
Turkey on the outbreak of the Crimean war, and
was present at the battles of Alma, Inkermann, and
Balaklava.   He served on the staff of Lieutenant-
General Sir John Burgoyne during the siege of
Sebastopol, was promoted for his services to a majo-

rity, and afterwards joined the 3rd Buffs, with which regiment he is at present serving in the Mediterranean.

The second son, James Thomas Burke, also entered the army at an early age. A clever mathematician and skilful engineer, a high-spirited and daring soldier, brave even to a fault, he lost his life at the battle of Giurgevo, on the Danube, on the 7th of July, 1854. Having, as a lieutenant of Engineers, accompanied Sir John Burgoyne to the seat of war, previous to the embarkation of the British expedition for the East, he assisted Omar Pasha in making arrangements for the defence of Silistria,* and being, like his countryman BUTLER, a volunteer in the service of the Sultan, entered that place among the gallant bands by whom it was afterwards so bravely defended. When the siege was raised, he joined Hussein Pasha at the fortress of Rustchuk, and strongly remonstrated with that general on his projected attack on the posts near Giurgevo, on the grounds that for certain obvious strategical reasons, the Russians must speeedily evacuate the town without causing any expenditure of life or labour. The hot-headed Hussein, however, who directed the operations from behind the walls of Rustchuk, decided on making the assault, and the brave Burke, like a gallant soldier, having first performed his duty in pointing out the rashness of the measure, imme-

* Nolan's *History of the Russian War.*

diately threw his whole soul into the work. The
following account of his heroic death is taken from
Russell's *History of the Crimean War :—*

"When he first leaped on shore from the boat, six soldiers
charged him. Two he shot with his revolver, one he cut
down with his sword, the rest turned and fled. ·While he
was encouraging the Turks who were in the stream to
row quietly to the land, and forming them in line as they
disembarked, conspicuous as he was in full uniform and
by his white cap cover, a number of riflemen advanced
from behind a ditch and took deliberate aim at him. He
charged them with headlong gallantry, and, as he got near,
was struck by a ball, which broke his jawbone; but he
rushed on, shot three men dead at close quarters, and
cleft two others, through helmet and all, into the brain,
with his sword. He was then surrounded, and while
engaged in cutting his way with heroic courage through
the ranks of the enemy, a sabre-cut from behind nearly
severed his head from his body, and he fell dead, covered
with wounds, of which thirty-three, consisting of sabre-
gashes, lance and bayonet thrusts, blows from the butts of
muskets, and bullet-holes, were afterwards found on his
body."

He was the first British officer killed in the Russian
war. Two Sappers, who were with him, stood by
him to the last, but were afterwards swept away, with
hundreds of others, before the walls of Sebastopol.
One of these, Anderson, a most distinguished soldier,
recovered the dead body of his officer on the morning
after the battle, at the imminent peril of his own life,

and was rewarded by Omar Pasha with the Order of the Medjidie for his heroic conduct.

The third son, ROBERT O'HARA BURKE, was born in 1821, and commenced his career as a cadet of the Woolwich Academy, but left it to enter upon a higher course of studies in Belgium. He afterwards entered the Austrian service as cadet in the Seventh Reuss Regiment of Hungarian Hussars, and at an early period obtained his lieutenancy. Quitting this service, he procured an appointment in the Irish Constabulary in 1848, and was almost adored by the men of that force, several of whom sent in their resignations when he left, and proceeded to Australia, that they might have an opportunity of continuing to serve under him. As another instance of the re-markable attachment he was accustomed to inspire in those connected with him, it may be mentioned that a woman named Ellen Doherty, of the age of sixty-five years, who had been his nurse, and whose heart yearned with a longing to see her " dear Master Robert," as she still continued to call him, left her comfortable home near the family seat of St. Clerans, in the county of Galway, where she had been well cared for as an old retainer of the family, and, unknown to any one, making use of the savings accumulated to sustain her in her old age, travelled, unprotected, alone, with the best feelings of her heart clinging close round him, to try and see her darling once more before she died. Alas! that meeting was never to take place in this world. She reached Melbourne after he had set out on the expedition from which he never returned alive.

It is pleasant to know that her case excited the greatest sympathy in Australia, and that provision was afterwards made for her comfortable support by the Government of the colony.

Mr. Burke emigrated in 1853, and was soon appointed acting inspector of police in Melbourne, whence he was transferred to a command at Carlsruhe, being soon after advanced to the Beechworth district, to relieve Mr. Price, the police magistrate, with promotion to the post of district inspector. On the news of the Crimean war he hastened home, on leave of absence, in the hope of getting a commission; but finding himself too late to share in the glories of the campaign, he returned to resume his Australian duties, in the discharge of which he rendered himself most popular. In 1858 he was removed to Castlemaine, and was comfortably stationed there, when he applied for and obtained the appointment of Leader of the Victorian Exploring Expedition.

From the moment it became probable that he would be selected to fill this responsible post, Mr. Burke is said to have diligently prepared himself for it, by devoting himself, with his habitual energy, to qualifying for it in every possible way. He at once commenced an active examination of

the records of previous explorers, so as to become
thoroughly acquainted with whatever had befallen
them, as well as to acquire such knowledge of the
interior, and remote coasts, as had already been
placed on record.   He had been at all times an
accomplished and daring horseman, and now entered
upon a course of severe pedestrian exercise, accustom-
ing himself to fatigue and privation of every possible
kind that an attempt to traverse the vast untrodden
wilds of Central Australia was likely to bring to his
experience.

CHAPTER III.

Formation of the Exploring Party—Exploration Fund Committee—
Public Dinner to Mr. Burke.

MR. BURKE's appointment was immediately followed
by the selection of the other members of the Expedition.   Mr. G. J. Landells, who had originally been
entrusted with the importation of the camels, and
who had carried out the duties confided to him in the
most successful and satisfactory manner, was offered
the post of second in command, with the view of
securing the aid of his personal superintendence in
the management of animals, which had been provided
at great expense, and from which much was expected.
One circumstance connected with this appointment
speaks so strongly to the high feeling and utter
abnegation of personal interests displayed by Mr.
Burke at this period, that it may be fitly mentioned
here, to the honour of one of the most active and
energetic men ever employed on an expedition of
difficulty and danger.   It is this: when Mr. Landells'
salary, which it was proposed to fix at a certain rate,
was, on inquiry, found to be higher than that allotted
to Mr. Burke, the committee at once saw the neces-

sity of augmenting the leader's salary to a greater, or, at least, equal amount. This, however, Mr. Burke firmly declined: cordially supporting the proposition in favour of Mr. Landells, he said that gentleman's services ought to be secured at his own price or not at all, and that he cared nothing for money himself. How far this frank and manly course operated in setting an example of subordination and forbearance to Mr. Landells at a later period, when his adherence began to be of importance, will be seen from the sequel.

The third officer of the expedition was Mr. William John Wills, of the Melbourne Observatory. This gentleman—whose patience, perseverance, and noble fidelity to his leader, never at any time forsook him, and whose name is immortalized as Burke's faithful companion in danger and in death—shares with his heroic chief the honour of being the first to cross the Australian continent from sea to sea. He was born at Totness, Devonshire, in 1834, and, being destined for the medical profession, studied at St. Bartholomew's Hospital, and distinguished himself as a student in chemistry. He arrived in Australia in 1852, where, after some years spent with his father in the practice of medicine, during which time he had displayed a taste for, and great ability in the study of, astronomy and meteorology, he was at length nominated to the staff of the Observatory in Melbourne. He applied to join the Expedition, which he did at considerable pecuniary sacrifice, and was at once appointed astronomical and meteorological observer, and third in command.

Doctor Herman Beckler was appointed medical adviser, and botanist to the expedition.

Doctor Ludwig Becker was also attached to it as artist, naturalist, and geological director.

The following were engaged as foremen and assistants in subordinate capacities :—Messrs. Ferguson and Hodgkinson, William Brahé, John King, William Patten, Charles Gray, Thomas F. MacDonough, Dost Mohammed, a sepoy, and two natives, named respectively Belooch and Botan : there were fifteen persons in all.

The original committee, which at first belonged exclusively to the Royal Society of Victoria, had latterly become amalgamated with another body, selected at a public meeting for the purpose of raising subscriptions, under the name of the " Exploration Fund Committee." These two, when united, took charge, with the consent of the Government, of all subsequent proceedings, and were presided over by the Hon. Sir William F. Stawell, Chief Justice of the colony, as Chairman.

The other members were:— The Hon. John Hodgson, M.L.C., Vice-Chairman ; Mr. Ligar, the Surveyor General ; Mr. Hodgkinson, the Deputy Surveyor General ; Professor M‘Coy ; Professor Neumayer ; Dr. Mueller ; Captain Cadell ; Mr.

Selwyn; Rev. Mr. Bleasdale; Dr. Gilbee; Dr. Eades; John Watson, Esq.; Angus M'Millan, Esq.; Dr. Iffla; Sizar Elliott, Esq.; Dr. MacKenna; James Smyth, Esq.; Dr. Embling. The Hon. Dr. Wilkie, Treasurer; and the Hon. Dr. M'Adam, M.P., as Secretary.

These gentlemen, having completed the appointment of the different officers of the expedition, &c., lost no time in providing the necessary stores and means of transport; and several members of the committee, among whom was Sir William Stawell, assisted Mr. Burke in the selection of the various matters necessary to be provided for that purpose. Large quantities of dried meat, flour, biscuit, sugar, forage for the camels and horses, as well as an abundant supply of veterinary and other medicines, were supplied, to the value of nearly 5,000*l*.; these were calculated to last for twelve months, and were not intended to be trenched upon while the party remained within the bounds of civilization. Nothing that the most anxious care could suggest, to provide for the comfort and safety of the explorers, was omitted; and the most competent authorities in every branch of scientific inquiry, regardless of time and trouble, vied with each other in exerting themselves to give all the assistance and information possible, so as to render the expedition which Mr. Burke commanded one of the best equipped bodies that had ever been organized for such a purpose.

The astounding and heart-rending fact that these abundant stores were withheld from the bravest spirits of the party in their hour of greatest need, and the name of the individual responsible for the fatal neglect, will appear in its proper place hereafter, to the shame and everlasting disgrace of the unhappy man who accepted and betrayed his leader's sacred trust.

Mr. Burke did not leave the scene of his previous duties without receiving from the inhabitants of Castlemaine abundant proofs of their attachment to him, as well as of the high estimation in which his services were held. On Friday, July 6th, 1860, a large and influential assemblage sat down to a public dinner given in his honour, at which it was found impossible to furnish room for all the persons who wished to attend to bid their guest a kind farewell and wish him God speed. To assist in preserving the record of scenes which have acquired a mournful interest from Mr. Burke's sad fate, a brief account of what then took place is here transcribed, with a summary of some of the speeches delivered by the principal speakers on the occasion.

The chair was filled by William Froomes, Esq., president of the Municipal Council. W. B. Collyns, Esq., and Dr. Preshaw officiated as croupiers; and all classes of the community were ably represented by men most anxious to give expression to the unbounded enthusiasm which prevailed. After the usual loyal toasts had been given and responded to, the Chairman rose to propose the toast of the evening. He remarked upon the cordial demeanour, urbane and frank manner, and numerous sterling qualities of their honoured guest, and bore testimony to the humanity and discrimination with which he had performed many unostentatious acts of kindness while stationed among them. In thus giving expression to the sentiments of all, it became his duty publicly to assure Mr. Burke that, in his glorious undertaking as leader of the explorers, the prayers and best wishes of a thousand hearts would follow and accompany him; and that, while they regretted the loss they suffered in being deprived of his presence there, they yet felt a pride in the reflection that the man who they believed was destined to penetrate and explore the pathless wilds of Central Australia had some time lived among them, and would at some future period remember, perhaps with pleasure, the parting hours he had spent with his friends that day.

The Rev. J. Storie also rose to say a few words. A brave man whom they all esteemed was going forth on an enterprise of national importance and great peril, and they had met to wish him with all their hearts " God speed." If there really existed within their great continent a Sahara—a desert of sands, parent of hot winds—they should like to know the fact. If great lakes, on whose verdant banks thousands of cattle might feed, or watered plains which might tempt men to build new cities, let them know the character and promise of the land, by the true report of a true man. As in the ancient days of Bible story brave men were sent to view the Land of Promise, so a gallant band now quitted them on a like errand, and he might assure his guest that while his best wishes accompanied him, he could also promise that his party would be followed by the prayers of *one* congregation at least, who would remember him before the throne of grace, and pray that he and his brave companions might be preserved from all peril, and having prospered in their enterprise, might come back, safe and triumphant, to be crowned with laurels by a grateful country.

Last of all, the meeting was eloquently addressed by Mr. Leech. He reviewed the history of exploration from the earliest times. He recognized in the energy of the Anglo-Saxon character a means made use of by Providence to bestow the blessings of civilization on millions of the human race. He pictured the rise and progress of future states within their vast continent, and trusted that the day would come when men of future generations, teaching their children, would say, " My son, the country in which we live was first opened to us by Robert O'Hara Burke."

When Mr. Burke rose to respond, some time elapsed before the enthusiasm of his admirers would allow him to make himself heard. He said he was about to make his first speech. He felt deeply the warm sympathy and hearty expressions of good-will with which he had that evening been honoured, and knew it was unnecessary for him to say how he appreciated the kind and generous feeling which led those present to encourage a man who found himself appointed to an arduous and difficult position. He had used every fair, honourable, and straightforward means to secure his post. Like all other men under similar circumstances, he had had his detractors, but he hoped that his future conduct would be to these a sufficient answer. With heartiest thanks to all who had been kind to him, and to the people of Castle-maine particularly, he would cheerfully encounter his task, and he pledged himself to strain every nerve to bring the expedition to a successful issue.

And nobly he redeemed his pledge.

CHAPTER IV.

Departure of the Expedition—Journey to Menindie on the River
Darling—Landells withdraws from the Party—Mr. Burke's
difficult Position—Division of the Party—Measures for formation
of permanent Depôt in the Interior.

ON the 20th of August, 1860, the Expedition quitted
the Royal Park at Melbourne. Headed by Messrs.
BURKE, Landells, and WILLS, and amidst a burst
of popular enthusiasm which seemed to pervade all
classes, the heroic adventurers started on their perilous
mission. On the 24th the Expedition camped at Sand-
hurst, and on the following day proceeded *en route* to
Swan Hill, which it reached on the 6th of September;
and at this place it was most hospitably entertained
by the leading inhabitants prior to its taking leave of
the colony of Victoria. It then entered the adjoining territory of New South Wales, and proceeded
towards the Darling, a tributary of the Murray River,
into which the former flows about 120 miles south of
Menindie. At this last-named place Mr. Burke
established his first depôt. He reached it about the
23rd of September, and although the journey so far
had been easy, yet the whole of the stores had not
arrived.

A difficulty here arose with Mr. Landells, which led to that gentleman's withdrawal from the party. It would seem that Mr. Landells had laid such stress on the importance of the position he himself held in the expedition, that he was unable to control certain feelings of impatience at the exercise of authority on the part of Mr. Burke; although it was distinctly understood before the expedition left Melbourne that " no divided authority could be recognized, nor could the absolute authority of the leader be permitted to be called in question." * Indeed, it is difficult to conceive how any man in his senses could attempt to interfere with the absolute supremacy of command indispensably necessary in an enterprise of such danger and importance. At all events, as has been said, a difficulty arose. Mr. Burke, considering that some rum which had been brought up for the use of the camels endangered the sobriety of his men, decided on leaving it behind; but to this prudent measure Mr. Landells would by no means consent. Big with his own importance, and putting out of sight the necessity of implicit obedience to his chief, who was striving, at the peril of fame, fortune, and life, to fulfil the duty with which he had been entrusted; moreover, disregarding the possible evil effect of his withdrawal upon other members of the party, who, already growing faint of

* Letter from Professor M'Coy to Mr. Landells, dated 24th November, 1860.

2—2

heart, only sought a decent opportunity of retiring from their posts; and influenced himself, it was afterwards publicly suggested, by feelings of misgiving, Mr. Landells resigned. Whatever may have been his views with regard to the necessity of supplying rum to the camels, two things are certain—One, that these animals *did* most effectively perform their work subsequently without the administration of any spirituous liquor—the disease from which they chiefly suffered (the scab) being cured, not by the use of rum, but by the application of an ointment composed of brimstone and grease; the other, that his withdrawal immediately led to the resignation of the medical officer of the expedition. Thus Mr. Burke was placed in a position of the gravest difficulty at the very moment when the actual dangers of the exploration commenced, and which required to be met with unity of purpose, firmness, and decision.

Although Mr. Burke was thus suddenly deprived of the services of two persons upon whom he was justified in relying for cordial assistance and zealous support, he did not suffer the circumstance to interfere with the vigour of his action, or his prompt execution of the duties he had undertaken to perform. The following extract from a letter written by him to his sister at this time will show how soon dangers and difficulties began to beset him, and how resolutely and courageously they were encountered :—

I received your letter, and have read it over and over again. It has been the greatest relief to my mind from dwelling on the difficulties and obstacles which obstruct me in the arduous task I have undertaken. I am waiting here for some stores I was obliged to leave behind; but if I wait too long my horses will grow mad from eating an herb which grows upon the river, so that I am not in the most pleasant position in the world, even at present.

I long to see you, the more, now that it is likely to be so long before we meet again ; but if I accomplish my task, I will go straight home to receive your congratulations in person. I am *confident* of success, but know that failure is possible; and I feel that failure would, to me, be ruin; but I am determined to succeed, and count on completing my work within a year at farthest.

Accepting, then, in its widest sense, the responsibilities of his position, Mr. Burke immediately set himself to look for fit persons to replace those who had forsaken him, and at once promoted Mr. Wills to the post of second in command. He afterwards met with a Mr. Wright, who volunteered to show the party a practicable route towards Cooper's Creek, four hundred miles farther on, where it had been decided to establish a permanent depôt; although different settlers and gentlemen on the river had endeavoured to persuade Mr. Burke that it was not possible to get there at that season of the year. On this point, however, Mr. Burke determined to be satisfied by immediately putting himself in front at the post of danger, examining the route, and testing the degree of dependence that might be placed on Mr. Wright's promises. To avoid, however, compromising the safety of the whole party by rashly entangling them, encumbered with heavy baggage, in the mazes of an unknown country, without any reserve, he requested Dr. Beckler to remain at Menindie in charge of the heaviest portion of the stores until arrangements could be made to forward them to Cooper's Creek. To this the doctor readily consented; for, though unwilling to accompany the party beyond the settlements, he had no objection to continue his employment under safe circumstances. Mr. Burke accordingly divided the Expedition into two parts, one to act with himself as an exploring party under Mr. Wright's guidance, the other to remain with Dr. Beckler until measures should be completed to send them on for the establishment of a permanent depôt in the interior.

CHAPTER V.

THE following paragraphs, from the written instructions issued to Mr. Burke by the Exploration Committee, under date 18th of August, 1860, may properly be inserted here :—

The Committee, having decided upon " Cooper's Creek " of Sturt as the basis of your operations, requests that you will proceed thither, form a depôt of stores and provisions, and make arrangements for keeping open a communication in your rear to the Darling, if in your opinion advisable, and thence to Melbourne, so that you may be enabled to keep the Committee informed of your movements, and receive in return the assistance in stores and advice of which you may stand in need. Should you find that a readier communication can be made by way of the South Australian police station near Mount Searle, you will avail yourself of that means of writing to the Committee.

Here follow suggestions as to certain routes recommended to Mr. Burke's notice, with the following addition, however :—

The Committee is fully aware of the difficulty of the

country you are called on to traverse, and in giving you
these instructions, has placed these routes before you, more
as an indication of what is deemed desirable to have
accomplished, than as dictating any exact course for you
to pursue.

The Committee considers that you will find a better and
a safer guide in the natural features of the country through
which you will have to pass.

For all useful and practical purposes, it will be better
for you, and for the object of future settlements, that you
should follow the watercourses and the country yielding
herbage, than to pursue any route which the Committee
might be able to 'sketch out from an imperfect map of
Australia.

The Committee entrusts you with the largest discretion
as regards the forming of depôts, and your movements
generally, but requests that you will mark your routes as
permanently as possible, by leaving records, sowing
seeds, building cairns, and marking trees at as many
points as possible, consistent with your various other
duties.   —

That Mr. Burke, in addition to the marking of
trees, &c., *had* various other duties claiming his personal superintendence, as foreseen by the Committee,
is worthy of note in this place, and the reader is
requested to remember it.

The exploring party, under Mr. Wright's guidance,
left Menindie on the 19th of October; and the following despatch, written by Mr. Burke from Torowoto,
about two hundred miles farther on, will show the
fair reasons that existed for placing confidence in

Mr. Wright, as well as explain the arrangements made for preserving the communication with Melbourne:—

Torowoto, October 29, 1860.*

Sir,—I have the honour to report that I left Menindie on the 19th instant with the following party :—Messrs. Burke, Wills, Brahé, Patten, M'Donough, King, Gray, Dost Mohammed; fifteen horses and sixteen camels, and Mr. Wright, who had kindly volunteered to show me a practicable route towards Cooper's Creek, for a distance of a hundred miles from the Darling, and he has more than fulfilled his promise; for we have now travelled for upwards of 200 miles, generally through a fine, sheep-grazing country ; and we have not had any difficulty about water, as we found creeks or water-holes, many of them having every appearance of permanent water, at distances never exceeding twenty miles. Mr. Wills's report, herewith forwarded, gives all the necessary details. Although travelling at the rate of twenty miles a day, the horses and camels have all improved in condition ; and the country improves as we go on. Yesterday, from Waunomatea to Paldrumati Creek, we travelled over a splendid grazing country, and to-day we are encamped on a creek or swamp, the banks of which are very well grassed, and good feed all the way from our last camp (44) except for two miles, and here the ground was barren and swampy. Of course it is impossible for me to say what effect an unusually dry summer would produce throughout this country, or whether we are now travelling in an unusually favourable season or not. I describe things as I find them.

Mr. Wright returns from here to Menindie. I informed him that I should consider him third officer of the

* Received by Committee, 3rd December, 1860.

Expedition, subject to the approval of the Committee, from the day of our departure from Menindie, and hope that they will confirm the appointment. In the meantime I have instructed him to follow me up, with the remainder of the camels to Cooper's Creek, and to take steps to procure a quantity of salt meat; and I have written to the doctor,* to inform him that I have accepted his resignation, as, although I was anxious to await the decision of the Committee, the circumstances will not admit of delay, and he has positively refused to leave the settled districts. I am willing to admit that he did his best until his fears for the safety of the party overcame him; but those fears, I think, clearly show how unfit he is for his post. If Mr. Wright is allowed to follow out the instructions I have given him, I am confident that the result will be satisfactory; and if the Committee think proper to make inquiries with regard to him, they will find that he is well qualified for the post, and that he bears the very highest character. I shall proceed on from here to Cooper's Creek. I may, or may not, be able to send back from there until we are followed up; perhaps it would not be prudent to divide the party : the natives here have told Mr. Wright that we shall meet with opposition on our way there. Perhaps I might find it advisable to have a depôt at Cooper's Creek, and to go on with a small party to examine the country beyond it. *Under any circumstances it is desirable that we should be soon followed up.* I consider myself very fortunate in having Mr. Wills as my second in command. He is a capital officer, zealous and untiring in the performance of his duties; and I trust that he will remain my second as long as I am in charge of the expedition.

* Beckler.

The men all conduct themselves admirably, and they are all most anxious to go on; but the Committee may rely upon it that I shall go on speedily and carefully, and that I shall endeavour not to lose a chance, or to run any unnecessary risk.

I have, &c.

(Signed)   R. O'HARA BURKE, Leader.

P.S.—The two blacks and four horses go back with Mr. Wright.

The foregoing despatch proves that Mr. Burke had been at some pains to make inquiries respecting the man he had nominated as third officer of the Expedition. Mr. Wright had been for three years in charge of a cattle station on the river Darling, but had recently been thrown out of employment in consequence of a change of owners. He professed to have a knowledge of the country, and did really display such knowledge. In addition to this, he bore "the very highest character." Yet Mr. Burke has been blamed for trying to secure his services "without a previous personal knowledge of him!" and that, too, at a time when "a pressing urgency had arisen for the appointment, from the sudden resignations of Mr. Landells and Dr. Beckler." Besides, the Committee were aware of Mr. Wright's nomination on the 3rd December, and if they had had any objection to it, might even then have replaced him by another person in sufficient time to save the lives of the explorers by forwarding relief, as so distinctly requested by Mr. Burke. *He* did all in *his* power to make the arrangements as complete as possible; and had his directions been attended to, it is probable that not a single life would have been lost on the expedition. His object was to push on while the wet weather lasted, and while his party preserved the vigour of health and strength. Had he waited, squandering his time until the approach of the warm season, he would have found the supply of water dried up in many places, and his progress in consequence impeded and protracted, while at the same time both men and beasts would have grown more and more exhausted, and less able to perform their work. It is to the *rapidity* of Mr. Burke's progress that his ultimate success is due.

The following extract from Mr. Wright's report, who started one hundred days after his leader (nearly three months later than he should have done), will show how prudent Mr. Burke was in his calculations, and how correct his views were:—

The route followed by Mr. Burke at the period of his transit abounded in water: the rapidity with which he progressed afforded no opportunity to the natives of forming hostile combinations, and the men under his charge preserved their health.

But when I moved onwards from the Darling, the advance of summer had dried up nearly all the water-courses, and the ravages of scurvy reduced the effective strength of my party to an alarming extent.

Mr. Wright then, having escorted the party as far as Torowoto, took leave of them there on the 31st of October, bringing back with him two blacks and four horses, and having first received and engaged to carry out the following instructions:—" *To return to Menindie, and bring up the stores as rapidly as possible to Cooper's Creek.*"

In support of the fact that these instructions were plainly enough given, it may be said that the words themselves are taken from the evidence of the Honourable Dr. M'Adam before the Royal Commission (*Ans.* 19), and he afterwards adds (*Ans.* 613), " The Committee considered that Mr. Wright would unquestionably have left immediately."

Brahé states (*Ans.* 197) that Mr. Burke expected Wright at Cooper's Creek " within two days" from 16th December.

M'Donough states (*Ans.* 403) that Mr. Burke said to him on 15th December, " I expect Mr. Wright up in a few days—a fortnight at farthest. I left him *positive instructions* to follow me."

King states (*Ans.* 693) that on the 16th December Mr. Burke told the party " he then expected Mr. Wright daily."

Wright himself states in his evidence (*Ans.* 1,235), " I gave Mr. Burke my word that I would take the remainder of the party out as soon as I returned."

In his first despatch, also, to the Committee, Wright says, under date 19th December, " I have the honour

to inform you that, pursuant to a previous understanding with Mr. Burke, it was my intention to
rejoin that gentleman with the members of the party
and stores at present in this camp." And further
on: "As I have every reason to believe that Mr.
Burke has pushed on from Cooper's Creek, relying
upon finding the depôt stores at that watercourse
upon his return, there is room for the most serious
apprehensions as to the safety of himself and party,
should he find that he has miscalculated."

Yet this man, with such a dreadful conviction on his
mind, could bear to fritter away his time from the 5th
of November to the 26th of January, without doing a
single thing towards actually performing the impera-
tive though simple duty with which he had been entrusted! Mr. Burke's arrangements seem to have
been all that human foresight could suggest. Can
any reasonable person doubt that Wright knew perfectly well the exact nature of his instructions, and
foresaw the disastrous consequences almost certain
to ensue should they be disregarded?

CHAPTER VI.

GUIDED part of the way by three blacks, who had been procured at Torowoto, the explorers found no difficulty in reaching Cooper's Creek—a sort of inland lake or watercourse, about four hundred miles from Menindie. From the date of their leaving Melbourne, they had been in the habit of numbering each stage, or encampment; and these numbers, by the time they arrived at the Darling, had reached as far as thirty. Torowoto was numbered thirty-five, and the spot at which they first struck Cooper's Creek, on the 11th November, was marked as Camp fifty-seven.

They spelled (or rested) here one day, and then resumed their journey along the Creek, occasionally resting two days at a time, during which intervals Mr. Wills went out to feel the way before starting again. They formed their first depôt at Camp sixty-three, remaining there a fortnight. From this place Mr. Burke made a short trip northward with

Brahé; but not finding any water away from
the Creek, they were obliged to return the second
day.   Mr. Wills and M'Donough then went out,
taking three camels with them, and travelled
northerly for nearly ninety miles without finding
water.   On the third day they began to return; but
on encamping that night, the camels unfortunately
strayed away, and were lost.   Mr. Wills speaks of
the occurrence in the following extract from a letter
to my sister :—

Cooper's Creek, December 11, 1860.

MY DEAR BESSY,—This will probably be the last opportunity I shall have to write to you before I return, and I
will take the opportunity to do so.   You must excuse this
being written in pencil; it is troublesome writing in ink,
it dries up so confoundedly fast.   I enclose you some seeds
from the Australian desert.   Tell mamma she must excuse
me writing her : she must read this, and fancy it is hers
also.   I have not even time to write to my father.   The
journey has hitherto been but as a picnic party, but I
fear we shall have some heavier work soon.   I have had
a slight specimen of it lately.   I went out for a few days
to explore the country to the north-east, accompanied by
one man and three camels.   I had left the man in charge
of the camels while I went to make some observations.
When I returned I found the man had allowed the camels
to stray.   I tracked them for some distance, but found
they had gone homeward.   There was nothing for it but
to walk back, so we started at seven A.M. next day.   After
walking about ten miles we fortunately found some water,
and we continued on until eleven A.M.   We then rested,
as it is trying to travel with the heat 130° in the sun, and

112° in the shade. . . . We walked eighty miles in less than fifty hours, including stoppages. It is astonishing how a walk like this gives one a relish for a drink of water. For water such as *you* would not even taste, one smacks their lips as if it were a glass of sherry or champagne. We had but half a pint between us for the last twelve miles. We have no idea of being out for three years as I supposed. I calculate on being in Melbourne in August at farthest.

The following is M'Donough's account of the loss of the camels :—

When we came to the camp that evening the moon was rising, and Mr. Wills wanted to take an observation. I went to let out the camels. They were very much done up, and not inclined to feed. We were almost without water at the time. We had some in bags, but they were leaking, and when Mr. Wills was taking the observations, I let out the camels, and returned to cook our supper. Then Mr. Wills and I sat down to supper. I noticed the camels going into the scrub. I went and brought them back to within about thirty yards of our camp. They were not hobbled. Mr. Landells had left the hobbles, and said they were no use to them.* In about ten minutes I went to look after the camels. It was then dark. I could not find them, so called Mr. Wills, and we went in search of them. We searched until twelve o'clock at night, and could get no trace of them. We returned to camp. Mr. Wills laid down and had a short sleep, desiring me to call him at two o'clock in the morning, and to make a few johnny cakes. He said, " If we do not find

* This seems incorrect, for hobbles appear to have been subsequently used by the party.

3

the camels, and do not get back, we are lost." In the morning we went to a rise about fifteen miles off, which we reached a short time before day, thinking that we might see the camels coming down the valley. Mr. Wills looked through his opera-glass, but could see nothing of them. We walked back to our camp. We had a little bread and water. We did not like to light a fire for fear of the blacks, so we made up our swag.* I had a large Colt's revolver, and thirty-five pints of water in a goat-skin bag. Mr. Wills had three or four johnny cakes, a Trench's revolver, and a pocket compass. We proceeded towards Cooper's Creek, and in about seven or eight miles found a small pool of stagnant water, from which we drank a great deal, and filled the goat-skin bag. We then proceeded, walking eight hours and resting four, until we reached the creek. The last night we camped we had no water, as the bag leaked, and Mr. Wills and myself were very much done up, in consequence of carrying it.

After this Mr. Wills was obliged to go back with King, to recover the saddles and other things that were left when the camels strayed away.

Meanwhile, the depôt was removed two stages farther on, to Camp 65, in order to avoid the ravages of numbers of large rats which infested the first depôt, making sad havoc among the stores.

Early in December Mr. Burke made arrangements to solve the problem of crossing the continent from sea to sea, by proceeding to the Gulf of Carpentaria on the northern coast. To increase their stock of pro-

* Or burdens.

visions a horse was killed, and the meat "jerked:" that is to say, deprived of bone and fat, and dried in the sun. Subsequently to this, another of the horses broke his leg, and was shot, the flesh being added to the quantity previously dried. Mr. Burke then formed the following advance exploring party:— R. O'H. Burke, leader; W. J. Wills, John King, Charles Gray, six camels, one horse. Patten, M'Donough, Dost Mohammed, six camels, twelve horses, and the remainder of the provisions, were left behind in charge of Brahé, with instructions to remain at Cooper's Creek until the return of Mr. Burke's party, or until the provisions should run short, *and not to leave unless from absolute necessity.*

The following is the despatch written to the Committee at this time, and left with Brahé to be forwarded by the first opportunity :—

Cooper's Creek, December 13, 10 *o'clock.*

SIR,—I have the honour to report that the Expedition under my command left Torowoto on the 31st of October, and arrived at Cooper's Creek on the 11th November; men, horses, and camels well. The road from Torowoto to Wright's Creek is good, but from Wright's Creek to the point where we struck Cooper's Creek, it is in some places very stony, although not by any means impracticable. From the 11th of November we travelled slowly down the creek until the 20th of November, in order to recruit the strength of the animals. On the 20th we arrived at what I conceived to be an eligible spot for the depôt, and we remained there (Camp 63) until the 5th instant, when we

3—2

were driven out by the rats, and obliged to remove lower
down to the place from whence I now write (Camp 65),
and where I have permanently established the depôt.

The feed upon this creek is good, and the horses and
camels have greatly improved in condition; but the flies,
mosquitoes, and rats which abound here, render it a very
disagreeable summer residence.

From Camp 63 we made very frequent excursions, in
order to endeavour, in accordance with instructions, to find
a practicable route northward between Gregory's and
Stuart's tracts, but without success. Mr. Wills, upon one
occasion, travelled ninety miles to the north, without finding water, when his camels escaped, and he and the man
who accompanied him were obliged to return on foot,
which they accomplished in forty-eight hours. Fortunately, upon their return, they found a pool of water.
The three camels have not yet been recovered.

I am satisfied that a practicable route cannot be established in that direction, except during the rainy season,
or by sinking wells, as the natives have evidently lately
abandoned that part of the country for want of water,
which is shown by their having sunk for water in all
directions in the beds of the creeks.

I also think that it would be very desirable to establish
the route to Cooper's Creek, and from Cooper's Creek to
the north farther to the westward, as the eastern or upper
part of the Creek, up to Camp 63, runs through earthy
plains, which, even now arid in fine weather, are very
difficult to travel over, but in winter or during wet weather
they must be quite impassable for horses and cattle.

I have, therefore, left instructions for the officers in
charge of the party, which I expect will shortly arrive
here, to endeavour during my absence to find a better and

shorter route between the depôt (Camp 65) and Wright's Creek, or between the depôt and the Darling. I proceed on to-morrow with the party, to Eyre's Creek.* And from thence I shall endeavour to explore the country to the north of it in the direction of Carpentaria, and it is my intention to return here within the next three months at latest.

I shall leave the party which remain here under the charge of Mr. Brahé, in whom I have every confidence. The feed is very good. There is no danger to be apprehended from the natives if they are properly managed, and there is, therefore, nothing to prevent the party remaining here until our return, or until the provisions run short.

I did not intend to start so soon, but we have had some severe thunderstorms lately, with every appearance of a heavy fall of rain to the north; and as I have given the other route a fair trial, I do not wish to lose so favourable an opportunity.

We are all in good health, and the conduct of the men has been admirable. Mr. Wills co-operates cordially with me. He is a most zealous and efficient officer. I have promoted Mr. Brahé to the rank of officer. The position he is now placed in rendered it absolutely necessary that I should do so. He is well qualified for the post, and I hope the committee will confirm the appointment.

I have given instructions to Mr. Brahé to forward this letter by the first opportunity.

I have, &c.

R. O'HARA BURKE, Leader.

* Burke, Wills, King, Gray, six camels, and one horse.

CHAPTER VII.

The written Records of the Expedition—Diary kept jointly by
Messrs. Burke and Wills—Surveyor's Report on the Country
lying between Torowoto and Cooper's Creek.

IT now becomes necessary to advert to the written
records left by the exploring party.   These were
kept in the handwriting of Mr. Wills, who devoted
part of every evening to the compilation of a diary
in which the proceedings of the day were entered
and read over to Mr. Burke, who made any additions
or alterations he thought advisable.   Mr. Wills also,
in his capacity of surveyor, furnished to his leader,
for the information of the Committee, a detailed
account of the country through which they passed.
The paper referring to that part of Australia lying
between Torowoto and Cooper's Creek is here given,
and will be found a most interesting document, full
of valuable information, and useful as being expla-
natory of many allusions made in the diaries which
follow hereafter.

The accompanying map will show the course taken
by the expedition, as marked in the tracing referred
to by Mr. Wills:—

Camp 65, Depôt, Cooper's Creek,
December 15, 1860.

SIR,—I have the honour to place in the hands of our
Leader, for transmission to the Committee, my third report,
and a tracing showing the country traversed since my last
was written. I regret that I have been unable to devote
so much attention to either as I could have desired, but I
have no doubt the Committee will make due allowance for
my want of time, and the inconveniences attending the
execution of such work in our present position.

I have, &c.

WILLIAM J. WILLS,

The Honorary Secretary of the   *Surveyor and Assistant*
Exploration Committee.   *Observer.*

(Forwarded).   *Depôt, December* 16, 1860.

As Mr. Wills's report, with which I fully concur, contains all the necessary details with regard to the state of
the country through which we passed, I have not referred
to the subject in mine.

The Honorary Secretary of the   R. O'HARA BURKE,
Exploration Committee.   *Leader.*

SURVEYOR'S REPORT.

The accompanying tracing will show the course taken
by the expedition party from the Torowoto Swamp, in
lat. 30° 1' 30" S., long. 142° 36' E., to the depôt on
Cooper's Creek, Camp 65, lat. 27° 37' 8" S., long.
141° 6' E.

Water Supply between Torowoto and Wright's Creek.—
The country traversed to the north of the Torowoto Swamp,
and lying between that place and Wright's Creek, is neither

so well grassed nor watered as that to the south of the
swamp; the land falls considerably as far as Cangapundy,
and a great extent of it is subject to inundation. Nearly
all the water met with was thick and muddy; it was
obtained from small clay pans, most of which would probably be dry in three weeks. This applies to all the
places at which we found water, with the exception of
Cannilta, Cangapundy, and the four water-holes to the
south of Wright's Creek.

Cannilta.—Cannilta is a water-hole of good clear water
in a small rocky creek, which runs out on the low mud
flats and swampy ground lying between Altolka and
Tangowoko; it is situated in lat. 29° 26' 42" S., long.
142° 40' E. by account, nearly a mile from the north-
westernmost point of the swampy ground. This point
may be distinguished by the growth of a coarse kind of
reedy grass, which does not make its appearance on the
southern portion of the swamp or lake. The water in the
hole was only two or three feet deep, but is well shaded by
box-trees, and will probably last two or three months.
The temperature of the surface of the water at seven A.M.
November 2nd, was 60·5°, that of the air being at the
same time 60·0°

The Cangapundy Swamp.—The Cangapundy Swamp is
an extensive tract of low clay land, which bears the
appearance, as regards the vegetation on its banks, of having a tolerably permanent supply of water; but, unless
some portions of the swamp are much deeper than where
we passed, the water could not last throughout a dry
season. The banks of the swamp are densely clothed with
grasses, marshmallows, polygonum bushes, and shrubs,
which shelter numerous kinds of water-fowl and snakes.

Character of Land.—It will be seen by the tracing that

a large proportion of the land between Torowoto and Wright's Creek is composed of low mud plains and clay flats, subject to inundation. Most of these are devoid of vegetation of any kind, and others carry some stunted salt bushes and coarse grasses which appear to be struggling between life and death. Bounding the mud flats are generally some stony rises, well grassed, and sometimes lightly timbered. The more elevated plains are sandy, and support a fine supply of healthy salt bushes, as well as here and there a few grasses. On the rises to the S.S.E. of Cannilta may be seen great quantities of quartz rock, forming dykes in the schist rises; the latter in some places adjoin and run into hills of loose stone, having the appearance of indurated clay. From Cangapundy to Wright's Creek the ground is light-coloured, and of a clayey nature; it forms a series of dry clay-pans, separated from one another by low sandy banks on which the vegetation was fresh and green. At about seventeen miles from the former place are three large holes, with water from two to three feet deep in the deepest part, and at six miles farther on another large one, which might almost be termed a lake, being nearly 1,000 links square. About these were some lines of sand-hills running about northeast and south-west, and in one of the flats between the sand-hills I found several pieces of satin spar in lumps, the size of one's hand, partially buried in the ground, and all of them with the plane of cleavage nearly perpendicular to the surface of the ground.

Balloo or Wright's Creek.—The lower portion of Wright's Creek, called by the natives "Balloo," is situated in lat. 28° 48' S., and long. 142° 53' E. by account. At this point the creek, after breaking into several small channels, runs out on a grassy plain, the water continuing in a

southerly direction, probably until it meets that from the
Torrens and other creeks at the Cangapundy Swamp.
There was plenty of water in this part of the creek when
we passed, but I cannot speak to its permanence.   The
banks are well lined with box timber, as well as with marshmallows and wild spinach ; the land on either side consists
of well-grassed sandy rises.   At four or five miles above
this the creek is a narrow, dry, sandy watercourse, winding through a grassy valley, which everywhere presents
indications of the most violent floods.   Beyond this is an
extensive grassy plain, and for three or four miles scarcely
a trace of the creek could be seen.   We then came to a
clump of trees, amongst which were two large water-holes
surrounded by polygonum bushes, and containing great
numbers of small fish.   These holes appear to be permanent.   We found about sixty blacks camped here.   Above
these water-holes, which are together about half a mile
long, the creek again disappears on the plain.

The land for the next ten or twelve miles in a N.N.E.
direction is very fine for pastoral purposes, being alternately
grassy plains and sandridges.   At twelve or thirteen miles
we crossed the creek, where it has cut for itself a deep
narrow channel, the banks of which are densely timbered
and well grassed, but the water-holes are small and contained very little water.   For a distance of six miles the
creek is of a very insignificant character.   It appears to be
divided into several branches, which traverse clay flats badly
grassed.   Here and there are some lines of low sandy rises,
with plenty of feed on them.   All the watercourses are
distinctly marked by lines of box timber.   At about nine
miles from where we crossed the creek, and after traversing some loose polygonum ground which was covered with
mussel-shells and a shell resembling a periwinkle, we came

to a branch of the creek containing a splendid water-hole, 150 links broad and about half a mile long. A little above this the creek again disappears .for a short distance, and then there is a long narrow channel of undoubtedly permanent water, being nearly four feet deep in the shallowest places ; it is only on an average about fifty links broad, and well sheltered by overhanging box-trees. The temperature of the water on the morning of the 7th of November, at six o'clock, was 68°; the temperature of the air at the same time being 50·5°. Our camp at this place is indicated by a box-tree marked B over LII in square, the geographical position of which is by account 28° 26′ 9″ S. lat., and long. 148° E. In proceeding from here in a N.N.E. direction up the course of the creek, or rather of the water, for the creek is again lost on the plains for five or six miles, we passed the southernmost point of a prominent sandstone range, the nearest portion of which lay about a mile and a half to the westward.

At about nine miles we again touched the creek, where it is about three chains broad. The banks are firm and shelving, from ten to twelve feet above the water, and lined with box, acacias, some large gums, gigantic marshmallows, polygonum, &c. In the creek there is abundance of fish, and the ducks and other water-fowl on it are numberless. From what we have seen of the blacks, I should say the population cannot be far short of 150, and it might be considerably more. From here we proceeded in an E.N.E. direction along the west bank of this fine water-hole, and at two and a half miles found it begin rapidly to decrease in breadth, and a little farther on there was nothing but a few small stony watercourses traversing a dense box forest. At this point there is a level bed of sandstone pebbles, close to and over a part of which the creek flows. The blacks have here gone to the trouble of making paths for themselves, along which we turned off from the creek on a N.N.E. course, and at about three miles, coming on earthy plains, with no signs of water a-head, we again turned into the creek, and camped at a small water-hole. From here the line of river timber continues in a N.E. direction. To the W. and N.N.W. is a line of sandstone ranges running off in the same direction. The land in the immediate vicinity of the creek on the west side is very poorly grassed all the way up from where we crossed it; that on the east side appeared to be better.

I think there can scarcely be a doubt but what this creek is the lower portion of the Warrego River, although I believe that its main supply of water is obtained from the adjoining ranges, which send down innumerable creeks into the flats through which it flows.

Some latitude observations at Camp 53 (the farthest point to which we traced the creek) placed us in 28° 16′ 40″ S., our latitude, by account, being 28° 17′ 8″, and longitude 143° 18′ E. On Thursday, 8th November, we left Wright's Creek with the intention of crossing the ranges to Cooper's Creek. We found the land as we approached the hills well grassed, and in some places densely timbered; it is intersected by numerous water-courses, with deep sandy channels, in most of which there seemed little chance of finding water. We camped at a water-hole in M'Donough's Creek; the spot is indicated by a gum-tree marked B over LIV within square.

De Rinsy's Tracks.—Near here we found the tracks of drays; there were four distinct tracks, two of which appeared to be those of heavy horse-drays, the other two might have been made by light ones or spring carts; we

were unable to make out the tracks of the horses or cattle.
I cannot imagine what tracks these are, unless they may
be those of De Rinsy, who, I believe, had some drays with
him, and reported that he had been somewhere in this
direction. From Camp 54 to Camp 55, we were obliged
to take a very circuitous route, on account of the rugged
and stony nature of the ranges, which were more extensive
than we had anticipated; they stretch away far to the N.
and N.N.W., and although we kept well out to the N.W.,
we were unable to avoid the low stony rises which adjoin
them.

On the N.W. side of the hills we crossed two dry creeks
which flow in a N.N.E. direction ; their banks were thinly
lined with box-trees, and the holes in them were quite
dry. From this we took a W.N.W. course across undulating country covered with sandstone, quartz, and (magnetic) ironstone pebbles, so densely and firmly set together
in some places as to have the appearance of an old-fashioned
pavement. At about three miles we had to change our
course to N.W. to avoid a spur of the high range on our
left. At two miles farther we came to a grassy flat,
through which ran a fine-looking creek, but the bed was
sandy and quite dry; there were, however, a good many
small birds about here, which would indicate that there
must be water in the neighbourhood. We here again
changed our course to W.N.W., and at six miles camped
at a dry stony creek, having travelled about twenty-eight
miles over the worst ground that we had yet met with.
On the morning of the 10th we continued on a W.N.W.
course across stony ground of the same nature as that
passed during the previous day, but at a distance of five
miles we turned to W. $\frac{1}{4}$ S., as the ranges appeared to be
as low in that direction as in the other, and as they ran

nearly N.N.W., there seemed a chance of sooner getting
out of them, which we did at a distance of about eight
miles more.

From the point at which we emerged from these ranges,
the view was as follows:—From S.W. nearly up to N.W.
were extensive plains as far as the eye could reach, intersected by numerous lines of timber, the general direction
of which was about N.N.W.; several columns of smoke
were visible along these lines, some of which had the
appearance of camp and others of bush fires. From N.W.
to N. were lines of ranges running in a N.W. direction,
and in the valley between us and the first spur was a fine
line of timber, indicating the course of what appeared to
be a large creek, probably the recipient of all the small
creeks that we had crossed during the morning; in every
other direction there was nothing to be seen but timbered
sandstone ranges. At noon we crossed a small creek running nearly north; the grass had been burnt on its banks.
About half a mile beyond it was another creek of a more
promising appearance, and as we approached it we saw
several crows, as well as other birds in the trees. We
here found a small hole with the water fast drying up; it
contained a lot of young fish, about half an inch long, and
just sufficient water to replenish our water-bags, and give
the horses a drink; below it the creek took a N.N.W.
course, and was dry and sandy for a distance of two miles
and a half, at which point we found some large but shallow
holes of milky-looking water. On the plains near these
holes we found large flocks of pigeons; the grass was very
coarse and dry, and the water would probably not last
more than a few weeks.

Horse Tracks.—On the plains to the east of the creek
were the tracks of a single horse, which had evidently

crossed when the ground was very soft, and gone in a
S.W. direction.

Position of Water.—The water-holes are situated in
lat. 27° 51′ S., long. 142° 40′ E., by account from Camp 55.
From here a course of W. ½ S. took us in a distance of
about twenty miles to Cooper's Creek, which we first
struck in lat. 27° 49′ S., long. 142° 20′ E. The land
through which we passed on the 11th was so low and
wooded as to prevent me from seeing the direction of the
ranges; the first five or six miles was tolerably open; we
then came to a box forest, were the soil was loose and
earthy, similar to polygonum ground; there were in every
direction signs of heavy floods and frequent inundations;
we crossed several small water-courses, in one of which
there was a hole of rather creamy water, at which we
halted for an hour; from the water-hole we quite unex-
pectedly obtained a rather fine fish, about eight inches
long, of the same description as the young ones we had
found in Brahé's Creek.

Cooper's Creek.—At the point at which we first struck
Cooper's Creek it was rocky, sandy, and dry, but about
half a mile farther down we came to some good water-
holes, where the bed of the creek was very boggy, and the
banks richly grassed with kangaroo and other grasses.
The general course is a little north of west, but it winds
about very much between high sand-hills. The water-
holes are not large, but deep and well shaded both by the
steep banks and the numerous box-trees surrounding them;
the logs and bushes, high up in the forks of the trees, tell
of the destructive floods to which this part of the country
has been subjected, and that at no very distant period, as
may be seen by the flood-marks on trees of not more than
five or six years' growth.

From Camp 57 we traced the creek in a W.N.W. direction about six miles; it then runs out among the sand-hills, the water flowing by various small channels in a south-westerly direction. The main channel, however, continues nearly south until it is lost on an extensive earthy plain, covered with marshmallows and chrysanthemums.

Creek.—In one of the valleys between the sand-hills, at a distance of about ten miles in a S.W. direction, we found a shallow water-hole, where a creek is formed for a short distance, and is then lost again on the earthy plain beyond. W. by N. and W. from here, about twelve miles, there are some splendid sheets of water, in some places two and three chains broad; the banks are well-timbered, but the land in the neighbourhood is so loose and rotten, that one can scarcely ride over it. I expect this is the reason why we saw no blacks about here, for it must be worse for them to walk over than the stony ground. From Camp 60 the general course of the creek is N.W., but it frequently disappears on the earthy plains for several miles, and then forms into water-holes again finer than before. At our first depôt, Camp 63, in lat. 27° 36′ 15″ S., long. 141° 30′ E., there is a fine hole about a mile long, and on an average one chain and a half broad. It exceeds five feet in depth everywhere that I tried it, except within three or four feet of the bank. Two or three miles above this camp we saw the first melaburus growing around the water-holes, some of them as large as a moderate-sized gum-tree.

Earthy Flat.—The feed in the vicinity of Camp 63 is unexceptionable, both for horses and camels, but the herbage on the creek generally down to this point is of a very inferior quality; the grasses are very coarse, and bear a very small proportion to the other plants. By far the chief portion of the herbage consists of chrysanthemums and marshmallows; the former, to judge from their dried-up powdery state, can contain very little nourishment, although some of the horses and camels eat them with great relish; the latter, I need hardly mention, are at this time of the year merely withered sticks. A few small salsolaceous plants are to be found on some of the flats, but they are scarcely worth mentioning. In some places, where the bed of the creek is shallow and dry, there is an abundance of good grass and rushes of several kinds. The polygonum bushes are also fresh and good in such places.

Stony Rises.—The stony rises are generally bare and barren; but some of those on the north side of the creek carry a fair crop of light grass.

Sand-Hills.—Wherever there are sand banks or ridges, the feed is almost invariably good; the salt bush is healthy and abundant, and there are a variety of plants on which cattle would do well. For camels these hills are particularly well adapted, for there is scarcely a plant grows on them that they will not eat, with the exception of porcupine grass; but there is very little of that until one gets many miles back from the creek.

Character of Ground.—I have mentioned three distinct kinds of ground—the earthy plains, the stony rises, and the sand-ridges. The latter, which is by far the most agreeable, whether for travelling on, for feed, or in respect to the freedom from flies, ants, mosquitoes, and rats, is simply a series of hills composed of blown sand of a red colour, very fine, and so compactly set that the foot does not sink in it much; in some places the ridges have a uniform direction, in others the hills are scattered about without any regularity; the average direction of the ridges

4

is N.N.E. and S.S.W. In the valleys between the hills
are shallow clay pans, in which the water rapidly collects,
even after slight showers, but when full, they seldom
exceed five or six inches in depth, so that in summer they
are soon dry again.

Stony Rises.—The stony ground, in contradistinction to
the sandstone ranges, appears to have been formed from
the detritus of the latter, deposited in undulating beds of
vast extent. The greater portion of this ground appears
almost level when one is on it, but when viewed from a
distance the undulations are very distinct; the stones are
chiefly waterworn pebbles of sandstone, quartz, and ironstone; in some places the rises approach more nearly to
the nature of the sandstone ranges, and here the stones are
less waterworn, and are mixed with large blocks of rock.
I found the magnetic polarity to be very distinct in some
of the ironstone pebbles on these rises.

Earthy Plains.—The earthy plains, which are such an
important geological feature in this part of the country,
will, I fear, greatly interfere with its future occupation;
when dry, they are so intersected by chasms and cracks,
that it is in some places dangerous for animals to cross
them; and when wet, they would be quite impassable.
Cattle would, perhaps, do well on them for some time
after an inundation, and the ground might improve after
having been stocked. The boggy nature of the banks of
the creeks passing through this ground would be another
impediment to settlers, from the losses of cattle that it
would sometimes entail. To give one an idea of the danger
in that respect, I may mention, that there are places where,
for a distance of two or three miles, neither a bullock nor
a horse could get to the water with safety, and it was with
difficulty that we could approach it ourselves; the safest

spots are at the lower ends of the water-hole, where the creeks run out on the plains. A peculiar geological feature that I have never seen so strongly exhibited elsewhere is, that the watercourses on these plains have a strong tendency to work away to the south and south-west, the fall of the ground, as shown by the flow of the flood-water, being to the west and north-west. I found that at almost every place where a portion of the creek ran out, the small branches into which it split before disappearing struck off at nearly right angles to the creek, and that the flow of the water on the level plain was invariably in a westerly or north-westerly direction; whereas the creeks generally had a course considerably to the south of west, more especially before running out. The branch creeks and water-holes are always lined with box-trees and polygonum bushes; they are generally situated between or near sand-hills, and have doubtless been formed by the rush of water consequent on the interference of these hills with the general flow. In some places the direction of the sand-ridges was the course of the creeks, trending to the southward; but I allude to the tendency as exhibited on the open plain, with no sand-ridges near the creek.

Country to the North of Camp 63 (Cooper's).—During our stay at Camp 63, from which spot we found it necessary to remove for several reasons, but chiefly because the rats attacked our stores in such numbers that we could keep nothing from them, unless by suspending it in the trees, four excursions were made to the north of that place in search of a practicable route to the Gulf. The first attempt was made with horses, which were soon knocked up, from the strong nature of the ground and the want of water; the others we made by camels, by the help of

4—2

which the country was well examined to a distance of nearly ninety miles. Water was found at two places at distances of about seventy and seventy-three miles north of the creek, but it was fast drying up, and would not last beyond Christmas. No blacks were seen, but a column of smoke was observed to the N.N.E., at a distance of about fifteen miles, as ascertained by some bearings, from the point at which we turned back. The chief portion of the land traversed consists of land-dunes and flats of the same nature, the latter clothed with porcupine grass, the former with salt bushes, grasses, and a variety of shrubs, sometimes intermixed with mesembryanthemums and porcupine grass. The sandy ground is bounded on either side by sandstone ranges, from which numerous small creeks flow east and west until they are lost in small flats and clay pans amongst the sand-hills. Their course is marked by an acacia, which is somewhat analogous in its general characteristics to the common wattle; a few are favoured with some box-trees, but we only found water in one. The whole country has a most deplorable arid appearance; birds are very scarce, native dogs numerous. The paths of the blacks on the strong ground look as if they had not been used for many years. Ant-hills and beds are to be found everywhere in great numbers, and of considerable size; the paths to and from them are better marked and more worn than any I have seen before, but nearly all of them are deserted, and those that are inhabited contain a small and weakly population, that seems to be fast dying away. Neither about the flats nor the ranges did we see any signs of the heavy floods that have left such distinct marks in other parts, and the appearance of the whole country gave me the idea of a place that had been subjected to a long-continued drought. At the northernmost end of the eastern line of ranges, and on the west side of them, in lat. 26° 30′ S., long. 141° 40′ E., is a low detached line of range about seven miles from north to south. On passing inside this range at its southern extremity, one enters a flat bounded to the south by high red sand-hills, to the west and north by the low range, and running up to the N.N.E. until it reaches the main range. On the lower part of the flat there is no creek, but on proceeding up it at a mile and a half there are three water-holes, with a few bushes growing around them; the water was fast drying up when we were there. There were some ducks, snipe, and pigeons about them: the former always returned to the holes after having been disturbed, so I imagine there is not much more water in the vicinity. In continuing up the flat, the main creek appears to be that along which the box timber grows, but the bed is sandy and quite dry. By keeping off a little to the left, at a mile above the water-holes, one comes on the bed of another creek, with only here and there a gum-tree and a few bushes. Up this creek, at a distance of three miles nearly north from the three holes, and where the creek emerges from the ranges, is a large hole, well shaded by heavy box-trees; it contained only a small quantity of water when we passed, but I fancy that in ordinary seasons the water would be permanent. This creek has been much frequented by blacks at one time, but not lately. Hundreds of hawks and a good many crows and magpies were in the trees near the water-hole.

Geographical Position.—The geographical position of the three water-holes is by account from Cooper's Creek, lat. 26° 34′ south, long. 140° 48′ east.

Meteorological Remarks.—It would be rather premature for me to offer any opinion on the climate of Cooper's

Creek on so short a stay, and my other duties have prevented me from making any observations that would be worth forwarding in detail. I may mention, however, that neither on the creek, nor during the journey up, have we experienced any extreme temperatures; the heat, although considerably greater here than in Melbourne, as shown by a thermometer, is not felt more severely by us. The maximum daily temperatures since our arrival on Cooper's Creek have generally exceeded 100°; the highest of all was registered on November 27th at Camp 63, when the thermometer stood at 109° in the shade.   There was at that time a strong wind from the north, which felt rather warm, but had not the peculiar characteristics of a hot wind.   One of the most noticeable features in the weather has been the well-marked regularity in the course of the wind, which almost invariably blew lightly from the E. or S.E. soon after sunrise, went gradually round to the north by two o'clock, sometimes blowing fresh from that quarter, followed the sun to west by sunset, and then died away, or blew gently from south throughout the night. A sudden change took place yesterday, December 14th; the day had been unusually hot; temperature of air at one P.M. 106°, at which time circum clouds began to cross the sky from N.W., and at two P.M. the wind sprung up in the S.W., blowing with great violence (force 6); it soon shifted to south, increasing in force to (7) and sometimes (8); it continued to blow from the same quarter all night, and has not yet much abated; once during the night it lulled for about an hour, and then commenced again; it is now (four P.M.) blowing with a force of (5) from S. by E., with a clear sky.   Before the wind sprung up the sky had become overcast, and we were threatened with a thunderstorm; rain was evidently falling in the W.

and N.W., but the sky partially cleared in the evening without our receiving any. Flashes of distant lightning were visible towards the north; during the night the thunderstorm from the north approached sufficiently near for thunder to be distinctly heard : the flashes of lightning were painfully brilliant, although so far away. The storm passed to the S. E. without reaching us; the sky remained overcast until between eight and nine A.M., since when it has been quite clear; the temperature of air, which at sunrise was as low as 72°, has reached a maximum of 92·0° : it is at present 89·0°, and that of the surface of the water in the creek 78°. Two other thunderstorms have passed over since we have been on the creek, from only one of which we have received any rain worth mentioning.

Mr. Brahé, who remains here in charge of the depôt, and from whom I have received great assistance both in making meteorological observations and in the filling in of feature surveys, will keep a regular meteorological register. I have handed over to him for that purpose an aneroid barometer, No. 21,543, and four thermometers, two for dry and wet bulb observations, and the others for temperature of water, &c.

With regard to hot winds, the direction of the sand-ridges would seem to indicate a prevalence of east and west winds here rather than northerly.

WILLIAM J. WILLS,
Surveyor and Astronomical Observer.

Cooper's Creek, December 15, 1860.

CHAPTER VIII.

Wright's Inactivity and Disregard of Mr. Burke's Instructions—
His Inability to account for his Conduct.

THE advantage of attending to the rule of conduct
laid down in the precept, " Act, act in the living
present," was not, unfortunately, illustrated in the
conduct of Mr. Wright, whose proceedings, or rather
want of proceedings, will now be detailed.

As has been mentioned, Mr. Wright returned
to Menindie from Torowoto with " positive instructions " * to follow Mr. Burke and bring up the
remainder of the stores to Cooper's Creek.   The
poet's advice, however, indicates what Mr. Wright
ought to have done; and well would it have been
for his future reputation—not to speak of his peace
of mind—if, even at the eleventh hour, he had made
an attempt to bring up the smallest quantity of provisions to save the lives of two of the bravest and
most heroic men ever sacrificed by inexcusable apathy
and neglect.

Mr. Wright, with his promise to take out the
remainder of the party as soon as he returned still

* *Vide* Chapter V.

fresh upon his lips, reached Menindie on the 5th of November, 1860, and had he shown a tithe of the energy of his gallant chief, might have successfully performed all that was expected of him. He well knew, as has been already proved, that Mr. Burke depended entirely upon him for the means of keeping up a communication with the Darling and with Melbourne, and must have been aware of the fatal consequences almost certain to result to the advanced party if he neglected the instructions he had received. Time was then most precious : every day was of importance. He knew the nature of the country he had to pass, and the difficulty there was in going through it at a later season. He knew that Mr. Burke had gone up at the very latest period when he could probably succeed ; and yet from the 5th of November to the end of the following January he did absolutely nothing.

On his arrival at Menindie, Wright found a trooper named Lyons waiting with despatches for Mr. Burke, which contained information as to recent discoveries made by M'Douall Stuart, who had penetrated much farther into the interior than any previous explorer; the particulars of his progress having been forwarded by the Melbourne Committee for Mr. Burke's information. These despatches were, after a delay of five days, forwarded by the trooper who brought them, escorted by a native guide, and accompanied by a man named M'Pherson, who was required to

shoe the horses at Cooper's Creek.   On the way,
however, they knocked up their horses, lost their
road, and, after travelling far beyond their destina-
tion, only succeeded in being able to send back the
native with news of their sad plight; but they were
rescued from starvation by a party sent in search of
them near the end of December.

There was, however, nothing to prevent the reserve
party on the Darling from being formed and pushed
on to Cooper's Creek with at least a portion of the
stores; and had Mr. Wright paid the least regard to
the positive instructions he had received, he would at
once have done this, and have made use of the post-
office at Menindie to forward information of his movements to the Committee, who then could, and would,
have backed him up in the same manner as they
subsequently did, when alas! it was too late.   He,
however, strange to say, wasted precious time in
most shameful inactivity: making frequent trips to
see his family who were living twenty-one miles off,
suffering his party to spend their time uselessly in
what one of the witnesses called "knocking about,"
and allowing the precious days to slip unheeded by;
while his unaccountable conduct was notoriously a
matter of astonishment and comment to all the persons staying at Menindie at the time.

Wright's excuses for having acted in this manner are none of them satisfactory, and they all
appear to have originated in the man's excessive

timidity and want of energy. The slightest difficulty overcame him. He was, in fact, that great
object of contempt to the other sex—a coward.
He seems to have feared everything. He feared
that his appointment might not be confirmed
by the committee—that the animals he had (nine
camels and seven horses) would not be able to
carry up a "really serviceable quantity of provisions." He feared that his wife and family, who
were staying at the station he had lately been in
charge of, would not get safely and *comfortably* to
Adelaide, whither he wished to send them. When
at last, after unheard-of delays, he did make an
attempt to proceed, he was still haunted by the same
wretched faint-heartedness. He became afraid of
"the blacks," or that some of his men might die;
although he could hardly have expected that an
expedition of the kind could be carried on without
some casualties. "To make omelets, one must break
eggs;" and Englishmen are seldom accustomed to set
an undue value on their lives when employed on a
service of difficulty and danger.

But this would, perhaps, excite nothing beyond a
feeling of pity for the man, were it not that Wright's
prevarication before the Royal Commission compelled
the gentlemen who composed it to dismiss him from
their presence with disgrace, as a person who had con-
tradicted his own assertions, and rendered himself
unworthy of belief. He stated that he had written

a letter on his return from Torowoto to Menindie, forwarding Mr. Burke's despatch of the 29th of October, and requesting that his appointment as third officer of the expedition might be confirmed. But this letter, if written at all, never reached the Committee, and he had kept no copy of it. He stated that he wrote it himself, although all other papers forwarded by him were invariably written by another person in consequence of his imperfect education; and as his excuse of waiting for the confirmation of his appointment appears by evidence to have been an after-thought,* and was not put forward until nearly two months subsequently to his reaching Menindie from Torowoto, it may well be doubted whether his story of having written such a letter can be received with any degree of confidence. Certain it is that in other respects it is impossible to believe his statements, for in his first despatch to the Committee, dated the 19th of December, 1860, he says, "I delayed starting; merely because the camels left behind by Mr. Burke were too few in number, and too inferior in carrying powers, to carry out a really serviceable quantity of provisions;" yet in his examination before the Commissioners he stated that his principal reason was not that, but that he was waiting for the confirmation of his appointment; and on being pressed on more than one occasion to say how he reconciled these two statements, he was unable satisfactorily to

* Royal Commission, Questions 1638 and 1802.

do so. The two last questions put to him were answered as follows :—

Question 1702.—Then it is to be presumed that the Commission may consider that you have no answer to make to reconcile the statement in this despatch with your garbled statement made to the Committee?—I have no particular answer to make to that question.

Question 1703.—It should be pointed out to you, that unless you can answer that question satisfactorily, you stand in an awkward position before this Commission?— *No answer.*

The witness withdrew.

In fact, Wright was guilty of flagrant and most culpable neglect of Mr. Burke's instructions; for he never at any time forwarded the smallest quantity of provisions or clothing to Cooper's Creek, although the stores at his command were abundant, and sufficient means of transport quite within his reach. Even when he reached the place in company with Brahé, on the 8th of May, 1861, both men being mounted and having a spare pack-horse with them at the time, he did not bring even a morsel of bread or a cup of cold water to help the poor sufferers then pining away for lack of food in the wilderness in the very hour of their victory! Of the grave responsibility resting upon him, it is needless to say another word here.

CHAPTER IX.

Departure for Carpentaria—Diary of the Explorers.

On the morning of the 16th of December, 1860, Mr. Burke assembled the whole of the party at Cooper's Creek, and formally appointed Brahé to remain as officer in charge of the depôt until Wright's arrival. He then shook hands with the different men, one of whom (Patten), much disappointed at not being taken on with his leader, shed tears; and, indeed, the whole of the party were anxious to go on. But there was no complaining. All were in excellent health and good spirits, and the advance party were accompanied to their first camp, twenty-two miles down the creek, by Brahé, who was desired to await his leader's return at Cooper's Creek, until obliged to leave "by absolute necessity." These are the words employed in Mr. Wills's last letter to his father,* written and read over to Mr. Burke and King, by whom they were certified as correct, when all three began to feel that their last chance of life was rapidly passing away.† There can, therefore, be little doubt that, whatever the precise words may

* Royal Commission, Question 318.   † *Ibid*, Question 1069.

have been in which the instructions were given, considerable pains were taken, both before Mr. Burke's departure, and during the first day's journey, to impress upon Brahé that he was not to leave Cooper's Creek to return to the Darling, until the return of the exploring party from Carpentaria. It has been stated that, although the provisions taken on were only calculated to last for three months, yet a period of four months' absence was alluded to as quite possible; and this was impressed by Mr. Wills upon Brahé, with a request that four months might be allowed to pass before he quitted the depôt. In justice to Brahé, it is only right to say that he *did* actually remain more than four months; though at the same time it was in his power to have waited much longer.

On first starting, the party were well supplied with food, the following being the average daily ration: one pound of damper (a kind of bread), three-quarters of a pound of dried meat, and a quarter of a pound of salt pork; besides which about a quarter of a pound of rice for each was boiled every second day.

Their entire stock was as follows:—About 300 lbs. of flour, 110 lbs. of dried meat, 30 lbs. of meat biscuit, 90 lbs. of salt pork, 50 lbs. of oatmeal, 50 lbs. of sugar, 50 lbs. of rice, 12 lbs. of tea, 5 lbs. of salt; a few tins of preserved vegetables, and some butter. In addition to these provisions, it was found that the country through which they travelled supplied them with a leafy and nutritious vegetable called portulac, which proved a great assistance to the party in eking out their limited supply of rations.

King conducted the six camels; Gray led the horse, which he was often allowed to ride after he began to complain of illness. Messrs. Burke and Wills walked ahead, steering, in turn, by means of a pocket compass; and, in halting at night, the former was always particular in selecting, above all things, a good place for the camels to feed.

The details of the successful journey of these strong men are given, as follows, in the diary of the party. The Diary, written daily, with few exceptions, by Mr. Wills, was subsequently transcribed under the superintendence of Dr. Mueller, one of the members of the Committee of the Royal Society. Apart from the special interest attaching to the actual writing left by the explorers, the story cannot be better told than in the truthful and graphic language of the amiable, accomplished and heroic man who wrote it, under circumstances of the most difficult and trying nature.

COOPER'S CREEK TO CARPENTARIA.[*]

Field-book, No. 1.

Sunday, December 1860.—The two horses having been shod, and our reports finished, we started at 6.40 A.M., for

---

[*] The omissions in the diary are supplied as far as possible by the information contained in the Maps.

Eyre's Creek, the party consisting of Mr. Burke, myself, King, and Charley,* having with us six camels, one horse, and three months' provisions. We followed down the creek to the point where the sandstone ranges cross the creek, and were accompanied to that place by Brahé, who would return to take charge of the depôt. Down to this point the banks of the creek are very rugged and stony, but there is a tolerable supply of grass and salt bush in the vicinity. A large tribe of blacks came pestering us to go to their camp and have a dance, which we declined. They were very troublesome, and nothing but the threat to shoot them will keep them away; they are, however, easily frightened, and, although fine-looking men, decidedly not of a warlike disposition. They show the greatest inclination to take whatever they can, but will run no unnecessary risk in so doing. They seldom carry any weapons, except a shield and large kind of boomerang, which I believe they use for killing rats, &c.; sometimes, but very seldom, they have a large spear; reed spears seem to be quite unknown to them. They are undoubtedly a finer and better-looking race of men than the blacks on the Murray and the Darling, and more peaceful, but in other respects I believe they did not compare favourably with them; for, from the little we have seen of them, they appear to be mean-spirited and contemptible in every respect.

Monday, December 17, 1860.—We continued to follow down the creek. Found its course very crooked, and the channel frequently dry for a considerable distance, and then forming magnificent water-holes, abounding in water-fowl of all kinds. The country on each side is more open than on the upper part of the creek. The soil on the

* Gray.

5

plains is of a light earthy nature, supporting abundance
of salt bush and grass. Most of the plains are lightly
timbered, and the ground is finer, and not cracked up,
like at the head of the creek. Left Camp No. 67 at ten
minutes to six A.M., having breakfasted before leaving.
We followed the creek along from point to point, at first
in a direction W.N.W. for about twelve miles, then about
N.W. At about noon we passed the last water, a short
distance beyond which the creek runs out on a polygonum
(*Polygonum Cunninghami*) flat; but the timber was so
large and dense, that it deceived us into the belief that
there was a continuation of the channel; on crossing the
polygonum ground to where we expected to find the
creek, we became aware of our mistake. Not thinking it
advisable to chance the existence of water a-head, we
camped at the end of a large but shallow sheet of water
in the sandy bed of the creek. The hole was about 150
links broad, and   * feet deep in most places. In most
places the temperature of the water was almost incredibly
high, which induced me to try it in several places. The
mean of two on the shady side of the creek gave 97·4°.
As may be imagined, this water tasted disagreeably warm,
but we soon cooled some in water-bags; and, thinking that
it would be interesting to know what we might call cool,
I placed the thermometer in a pannikin containing some
that appeared delightfully cool, almost cold in fact. Its
temperature was, to our astonishment, 78°. At half-past
six, when a strong wind was blowing from south, and
temperature of air had fallen to 80°, the lowest temperature of water in the hose, that had been exposed to the
full effect of evaporation for several hours, was 72°. This
water for drinking appeared positively cold, too low a

* *Sic* in original.

temperature to be pleasant under the circumstances. A remarkable southerly squall came on between five and six P.M., with every appearance of rain. The sky, how-ever, soon cleared, but the wind continued to blow in a squally and irregular manner, from the same quarter at evening.

Wednesday, December 19, 1860.—Started at a quarter-past eight A.M., leaving what seemed to be the end of Cooper's Creek. We took a course a little to the north of west, intending to try and obtain water in some of the creeks that Sturt mentioned that he had crossed, and at the same time to see whether they were connected with Cooper's Creek, as appeared most probable from the direc-tion in which we found the latter running, and from the manner in which it had been breaking up into small channels flowing across the plains in a N. and N.N.W. direction. We left on our right the flooded flats on which this branch of the creek runs out, and soon came to a series of sand-ridges, the direction of which was between N. ½ W. and N.N.W. The country is well grassed, and supports pienty of salt bush. Many of the valleys are liable to be inundated by the overflow of the main creek. They have watercourses and polygonum flats, bordered with box-trees, but we met with no holes fit to hold a supply of water. At about ten miles we crossed a large earthy flat, lightly timbered with box and gum. The ground was very bad for travelling on, being much cracked up, and intersected by innumerable channels, which con-tinually carried off the water of a large creek. Some of the valleys beyond this were very pretty, the ground being sound and covered with fresh plants, which made them look beautifully green. At fifteen miles we halted, where two large plains joined. Our attention had been

5 — 2

attracted by some red-breasted cockatoos, pigeons, a crow, and several other birds, whose presence made us feel sure that there was water not far off; but our hopes were soon destroyed by finding a clay pan just drying up. It contained just sufficient liquid to make the clay boggy. At ten minutes to seven P.M. we moved on, steering straight for Eyre's Creek, N.W. by N., intending to make a good night's journey, and avoid the heat of the day; but at a mile and a half we came to a creek, which looked so well that we followed it for a short distance, and, finding two or three water-holes of good milky water, we camped for the night. This enabled me to secure an observation of the eclipse of Jupiter's (I) satellite, as well as some latitude observations. The night was so calm that I used the water as a horizon, but I find it much more satisfactory to take the mercury, for several reasons.

Thursday, December 21 (20).—We did not leave this camp until half-past eight, having delayed to refill the water-bags with the milky water, which all of us found to be a great treat again. It is certainly more pleasant to drink than the clear water, and at the same time more satisfying. Our course from here, N.W. by N., took us through some pretty country, lightly timbered and well-grassed. We could see the line of creek timber winding through the valley on our left. At a distance of five miles there was a bush fire on its banks, and beyond it the creek made a considerable bend to the S.W. At two miles farther we came in sight of a large lagoon bearing N. by W., and at three miles more we camped on what would seem the same creek as last night, near where it enters to the lagoon. The latter is of great extent, and contains a large quantity of water, which swarms with wild-fowl of every description. It is very shallow, but is surrounded by the most pleasing woodland scenery, and everything in the vicinity looks fresh and green. The creek near its junction with the lagoon contains some good water-holes, five to six feet deep. They are found in a sandy alluvium, which is very boggy when wet. There was a large camp of not less than forty or fifty blacks near where we stopped. They brought us presents of fish, for which we gave them some beads and matches. These fish we found to be a most valuable addition to our rations. They were of the same kind as we had found elsewhere, but finer, being nine to ten inches long, and two to three inches deep, and in such good condition that they might have been fried in their own fat. It is a remarkable fact, that these were the first blacks who have offered us any fish since we reached Cooper's Creek.

Friday, December 21.—We left Camp 70 at half-past five A.M., and tried to induce one or two of the blacks to go with us, but it was of no use. Keeping our former course, we were pulled up at three miles by a fine lagoon, and then by the creek that flows into it; the latter being full of water, we were obliged to trace it a mile up before we could cross. I observed on its banks two wild plants of the gourd or melon tribe; one much resembling a stunted cucumber; the other, both in leaf and appearance of fruit, was very similar to a small model of a water melon (probably *Muckia micrantha*). The latter plant I also found at Camp 68. On tasting the pulp of the newly-found fruit, which was about the size of a large pea, I found it to be so acrid that it was with difficulty that I removed the taste from my mouth. At eight or nine miles from where we crossed the creek we passed another large lagoon, leaving it two miles on our left, and shortly afterwards we saw one nearly as far on our right. This last we should have availed ourselves of, but that we expected to find water in a creek which we could see, by the timber lining its banks, flowed from the lagoon on our left, and crossed our course a few miles a-head. We reached it at a distance of four or five miles farther, and found a splendid water-hole, at which we camped. The creek at this point flows in a northerly direction, through a large lightly-timbered flat, on which it partially runs out. The ground is, however, sound and well clothed with grass and salsolaceous plants. Up to this point the country through which we have passed has been of the finest description for pastoral purposes. The grass and salt bush are everywhere abundant, and water is plentiful, with every appearance of permanence. We met with porcupine grass (*Triodia pungens*, Br.), and only two sandridges before reaching Camp 71.

COOPER'S CREEK TO CARPENTARIA.

Field-book No. 2.   Lat. 27° to 25½° S.   Stations 72 to 73.

Saturday, December 22.—At five minutes to five A.M. we left one of the most delightful camps we have had in the journey, and proceeded on the same course as before, N.W. by N., across some high ridges of loose sand, many of which were partially clothed with porcupine grass. We found the ground much worse to travel over than any we have yet met with, as the ridges were exceedingly abrupt and steep on their eastern side, and although sloping gradually towards the west, were so honeycombed in some places by the burrows of rats, that the camels were continually in danger of falling. At a distance of about six miles we descended from these ridges to undulating country of open box forest, where everything was

green and fresh. There is an abundance of grass and
salt bushes, and lots of birds of all descriptions. Several
flocks of pigeons passed over our heads, making for a
point a little to our right, where there is, no doubt, plenty
of water, but we did not go off our course to look for it.
Beyond the box forest, which kept away to the right, we
again entered the sand-ridges, and, at a distance of six
miles, passed close to a dry salt lagoon, the ridges in the
vicinity of which are less regular in their form and direction, and contain nodules of limestone. The ground in
the flats and clay pans near has that encrusted surface that
cracks under the pressure of the foot, and is a sure indication of the presence of saline deposits. At a distance of
eight miles from the lagoon, we camped at the foot of a
sand-ridge, jutting out on the stony desert. I was rather
disappointed, but not altogether surprised, to find the
latter nothing more nor less than the stony rises that we
had before met with, only on a larger scale, and not quite
as undulating. During the afternoon several crows came
to feed on the plain. They came from an E.N.E. direction,
no doubt from a portion of the creek that flows through
the forest that we left on our right. In the morning, as
we were loading, a duck passed over, but it was too dark
to see which way it went.

Sunday, December 23.—At five A.M. we struck out
across the desert in a W.N.W. direction. At four miles
and a half we crossed a sand-ridge, and then returned to
our N.W. by N. course. We found the ground not nearly
so bad for travelling on as that between Balloo and
Cooper's Creek; in fact, I do not know whether it arose
from our exaggerated anticipation of horrors or not, but
we thought it far from bad travelling ground, and as to
pasture, it is only the actually stony ground that is bare,

and many a sheep-run is, in fact, worse grazing than that.
At fifteen miles we crossed another sand-ridge, for several
miles around which there is plenty of grass and fine salt
bush. After crossing this ridge we descended to an earthy
plain, where the ground was rather heavy, being in some
places like pieces of slaked lime, and intersected by small
watercourses. Flocks of pigeons rose from amongst the
salt bushes and polygonum, but all the creeks were dry,
although marked by lines of box timber. Several gunyahs
of the blacks were situated near a water-hole that had
apparently contained water very lately, and heaps of grass
were lying about the plains, from which they had beaten
the seeds. We pushed on, hoping to find the creeks
assuming an improved appearance, but they did not, and
at one o'clock we halted, intending to travel through part
of the night; about sunset three flocks of pigeons passed
over us, all going in the same direction, due north by
compass, and passing over a ridge of sand in that direction. Not to have taken notice of such an occurrence
would have been little short of a sin, so we determined to
go eight or ten miles in that direction. Starting at seven
o'clock P.M., we, at six miles, crossed the ridge over which
the birds had flown, and came on a flat, subject to inundation; the ground was at first hard and even, like the
bottom of a clay pan, but at a mile or so we came on
cracked earthy ground, intersected by numberless small
channels running in all directions. At nine miles we
reached the bed of a creek running from east to west; it
was only bordered by polygonum bushes, but as there was
no timber visible on the plains, we thought it safer to halt
until daylight, for fear we would miss the water. At daylight, when we had saddled, a small quantity of timber
could be seen, at the point of a sand-ridge, about one and

a half to two miles to the west of us, and on going there we found a fine creek, with a splendid sheet of water, more than a mile long, and averaging nearly three chains broad; it is, however, only two or three feet deep in most parts.

Monday, December 24, 1860.—We took a day of rest on Gray's Creek, to celebrate Christmas. This was doubly pleasant, as we had never in our most sanguine moments anticipated finding such a delightful oasis in the desert. Our camp was really an agreeable place, for we had all the advantages of food and water attending a position of a large creek or river, and were at the same time free of the annoyance of the numberless ants, flies, and mosquitoes that are invariably met with amongst timber or heavy scrub.

Tuesday, December 25, 1860.—We left Gray's Creek at half-past four A.M., and proceeded to cross the earthy rotten plains in the direction of Eyre's Creek. At a distance of about nine miles we reached some lines of trees and bushes, which were visible from the top of the sand-ridge at Gray's Creek. We found them growing on the banks of several small creeks, which trend to the N. and N.N.W. At a mile and a half farther we crossed a small creek, N.N.E., and joining the ones above mentioned. This creek contained abundance of water, in small detached holes, from fifty to one hundred links long, well shaded by steep banks and overhanging bushes. The water had a suspiciously transparent colour and a slight trace of brackishness, but the latter was scarcely perceptible. Near where the creek joined them is a sand-hill and a dense mass of fine timber. The smoke of a fire indicated the presence of blacks, who soon made their appearance, and followed us for some distance, beckoning

us away to the N.E. We, however, continued our course
to the N.W. by N.; but at a distance of a mile and a half,
found that the creeks did not come round as we expected,
and that the fall of the water was in a direction nearly
opposite to our course, or about west to east. We struck
off N. ½ W. for a high sand-ridge, from which we anticipated seeing whether it were worth while for us to follow
the course of the creeks we had crossed. We were surprised to find all the water-courses on the plains trending
rather to the south of east; and at a distance of three
miles, after changing our course, and when we approached
the sand-hills towards which we had been steering, we were
agreeably pulled up by a magnificent creek, coming from
the N.N.W. and running in the direction of the fire we
had seen. We had now no choice but to change our
course again, for we could not have crossed even if we
had desired to do so. On following up the south bank of
the creek, we found it soon keeping a more northerly
course than it had where we first struck it. This fact,
together with its magnitude and general appearance, les-
sened the probability of its being Eyre's Creek, as seemed
at first very likely from their relative positions and directions. The day being very hot, and the camels tired from
travelling over the earthy plains, which, by-the-by, are not
nearly so bad as those at the head of Cooper's Creek, we
camped at one o'clock P.M., having traced the creek up
about five miles, not counting the bends. For the whole
of this distance, we found not a break or interruption of
water, which appears to be very deep; the banks are from
twenty to thirty feet above the water, and very steep;
they are clothed near the water's edge with mint and
other weeds, and on the top of each side there is a belt of
box-trees and various shrubs. The lower part of the

creek is bounded towards the north by a high red sand-ridge, and on the south side is an extensive plain, intersected by numerous water-courses, which drain off the water in flood time. The greater portion of the plain is at present very bare, but the stalks of dry grass show that after rain or floods there will be a good crop on the harder and well-drained portion, but I believe the loose earthy portions support no vegetation at any time. The inclination of the ground from the edge of the creek bank towards the plain is in many places very considerable. This I should take to indicate that the flooding is or has been at one time both frequent and regular.

Wednesday, December 26, 1860.—We started at five A.M., following up the creek from point to point of the bends; its general course was at first north by west, but at about six miles the sand-ridge on the west closed in on it, and at this point it takes a turn to the north-north-east for half a mile, and then comes around suddenly north-west. Up to this point it had been rather improving in appearance than otherwise, but in the bend to the north-west the channel is very broad, its bed being limestone rock and indurated clay, is, for a space of five or six chains, quite dry, then commences another water-hole, the creek keeping a little more towards north. We crossed the creek here and struck across the plain on a due north course, for we could see the line of timber coming up to the sand-ridges in that direction. For a distance of seven or eight miles we did not touch the creek, and the eastern sand-ridge receded to a distance in some places of nearly three miles from our line, leaving an immense extent of grassy plain between it and the creek. The distinctly-marked feature on the lower part of this creek is, that whenever the main creek is on one side of a plain, there is always a fine billybong on the opposite side, each of them almost invariably sticking close to the respective sand-ridges. Before coming to the next bend of the creek, a view from the top of a sand-hill showed me that the creek receives a large tributary from the north-west, at about two miles above where we had crossed it. A fine line of timber running up to the north-west joined an extensive tract of box forest, and the branch we were following was lost to view in a similar forest towards the north. The sand-ridge was so abrupt when we came to the creek, that it was necessary to descend into its bed through one of the small ravines adjoining it. We found it partially run out, the bed being sand, and strewed with nodules of lime, some of which were one and a half to two feet long. They had apparently been formed in the sand-downs by infiltration.

COOPER'S CREEK TO CARPENTARIA.

Field-book No. 3. Lat. S. 25½° to 23¾°. Station 78 to 85.

Tuesday, December 30, 1860.—Finding that the creek was trending considerably towards the east, without much likelihood of altering its course, we struck off from it, taking a ten days' supply of water, as there were ranges visible to the north, which had the appearance of being stony. A north-east by north course was first taken for about seven miles, in order to avoid them. The whole of this distance was over alluvial earthy plains, the soil of which was firm, but the vegetation scanty.

COOPER'S CREEK TO CARPENTARIA.

Field-book No. 4. Camp 85 to 90. Lat. 23¾° to 22¼°.
Fine country—Tropics.

Saturday, January 5, 1861.—On leaving Camp 84, we found slight but distinct indications of rain in the groves, and a few blades of grass and small weeds in the little depressions on the plain. These indications were, however, so slight, that but for the fact of our having found surface-water in two holes near our camp, we should hardly have noticed them. At a distance of about two miles, in a north-north-east direction, we came to a creek with a long, broad, shallow water-hole. The well-worn paths, the recent track of natives, and the heaps of shells, on the contents of which the latter had feasted, showed at once that this creek must be connected with some creek of considerable importance. The camels and horses being greatly in need of rest, we only moved up about half a mile, and camped for the day.

Sunday, January 6, 1861.—Started at twenty minutes to six o'clock, intending to make an easy day's stage along the creek. As we proceeded up in a northerly direction, we found the water-hole to diminish in size very much, and at about two and a half miles the creek ran out in a lot of small watercourses. At the upper end of the creek we found in its bed what appeared to be an arrangement for catching fish. It consisted of a small oval mud paddock, about twelve feet by eight feet, the sides of which were about nine inches above the bottom of the hole and the top of the fence, covered with long grass, so arranged that the ends of the blades overhung scantily by several inches the sides of the hole. As there was no sign of timber to the north, we steered off to north-west by north for a fine line that came up from the south-west, and seemed to run parallel with the creek we were about to leave. At a distance of about three miles we reached the bank of a fine creek containing a sheet of water two chains broad, and at least fifteen feet deep in the middle. The banks are shelving, sandy, and lightly clothed with box-trees

and various shrubs. On starting to cross the plains
towards this creek, we were surprised at the bright green
appearance of strips of land, which look in the distance
like swamps; on approaching some of them, we found
that there had been a considerable fall of rain in some
places, which had raised a fine crop of grass and portulac
(*Portulaca olerasca*, L.), wherever the soil was of a sandy
and light nature, but the amount of moisture had been
insufficient to affect the hard clayey ground, which con-
stitutes the main portion of the plain. The sight of two
native companions feeding here, added greatly to the
encouraging prospects; they are the only specimens of
that bird that I remember to have seen on that side of the
Darling.

Monday, January 7.—We started at half-past four A.M.,
without water, thinking that we might safely rely on this
creek for one day's journey. We, however, found the line
of timber soon begin to look small; at three miles the
channel contained only a few pools of surface water. We
continued across the plains on a due north course, frequently crossing small watercourses, which had been filled
by the rain, but were fast drying up. Here and there as
we proceeded, dense lines of timber on our right showed
that the creek came from the east of north. At a distance
of thirteen miles we turned to the N.N.E., towards a fine
line of timber. We found a creek of considerable dimensions, that had only two or three small water-holes; but
as there was more than sufficient for us, and very little
feed for the beasts anywhere else, we camped. I should
have liked this camp to have been in a more prominent
and easily recognized position, as it happens to be almost
exactly on the tropic of Capricorn. The tremendous gale
of wind that we had in the evening and night prevented

me from taking a latitude observation, whereas I had some good ones at the last camp and at Camp 86. My reckoning cannot be far out. I found, on taking out my instruments, one of the spare thermometers was broken, and the glass of my aneroid barometer cracked—the latter, I believe, not otherwise injured. This was done by the camel having taken it into his head to roll while the pack was on his back.

Tuesday, January 8.—Started at a quarter past five A.M., with a load of water, determined to be independent of all creeks and watercourses. At a mile and a half found surface water in a small creek, and at a mile farther water in two or three places on the open plains. The country we crossed for the first ten miles consists of fine open plains of firm argillaceous soil, too stiff and hard to be affected by the small quantity of rain that has fallen as yet. They are subject to inundations from the overflow of a number of small creeks which intersect them in a direction E.N.E. to W.S.W. Nearly all the creeks are lined with box-trees and shrubs, in a tolerably healthy state. Of the remains of dead trees, there is only a fair proportion to the living ones. After traversing a plain of greater extent than the rest, we, at ten miles, reached the creek, proportionately large and important looking. The channel, however, at the point where we struck it, was deep, level, and dry, but I believe there is water in it not far off; for there were some red-breasted cockatoos in the trees, and native parrots on each side. On the north side there is a part bearing off to the N.N.W. The mirage on the plain to the south of the creek was stronger than I have before seen it. There appear to be sheets of water within a few yards of one, and it looks sufficiently smooth and glassy to be used for an artificial horizon. To the

westward of the plains some fine sand-hills were visible,
nearly in the direction in which the creek flowed.   To the
north of the creek the country undergoes a great change.
At first there is a little earthy land subject to inundation.
The soil then becomes more sandy, with stony pans in which
water collects after rain ; the whole country is slightly
undulating, lightly timbered, and splendidly grassed.   A
number of small disconnected creeks are scattered about,
many of which contained water, protected from the sun
and wind by a luxuriant growth of fine grasses and small
bushes.   We passed one or two little rises of sand and
pebbles, on which were growing some trees quite new to
me ; but for the seed-pods, I should have taken them for a
species of *casuarina*, although the leaf-stalks have not the
jointed peculiarities of those plants.   The trunks and
branches are like the she-oak, the leaves like those of a
pine; they droop like a willow, and the seed is small, flat,
in a large flat pod about six inches by three-quarters of
an inch.   As we proceeded, the country improved at every
step.   Flocks of pigeons rose and flew off to the eastward,
and fresh plants met our view on every rise; everything
green and luxuriant.   The horse licked his lips, and tried
all he could to break his nose-string in order to get at the
food.   We camped at the foot of a sandy rise, where there
was a large stony pan with plenty of water, and where the
feed was equal in quality, and superior as to variety, to
any that I have seen in Australia, excepting, perhaps, on
some soils of volcanic origin.

Wednesday, January 9.—Started at five minutes past
five without water, trusting to get a supply of water from
the rain that fell during the thunderstorm.   Traversed six
miles of undulating plains covered with vegetation richer
than ever.   Several ducks rose from the little creeks as we

passed, and flocks of pigeons were flying in all directions. The richness of the vegetation is evidently not suddenly arising from chance thunderstorms, for the trees and bushes on the open plain are everywhere healthy and fresh-looking; very few dead ones are to be seen; besides which, the quantity of dead and rotten grass which, at present, almost overgrows in some places the young blades, shows that this is not the first crop of the kind. The grasses are numerous, and many of them unknown to me, but they only constitute a moderate portion of the herbage; several kinds of spurious vetches and portulac, as well as salsolaceæ, add to the luxuriance of the vegetation. At seven miles we found ourselves in an open forest country, where the feed was good, but not equal to what we had passed, neither had it been visited by yesterday's rain. We soon emerged again on open plains, but the soil being of a more clayey nature, they were not nearly so much advanced in vegetation as the others. We found surface water in several places, and at one spot disturbed a fine bustard which was feeding in the long grass. We did not see him until he flew up. I should have mentioned that one flew over our camp last evening, in a northerly direction. This speaks well for the country and climate. At noon we came to a large creek, the course of which was from E.N.E. to W.S.W. The sight of white gum-trees in the distance had raised hopes which were not at all damped on a close inspection of the channel. At the point where we struck it, there was certainly no great quantity of water; the bed was broad and sandy, but its whole appearance was that of an important watercourse, and the large gums which line its banks, together with the improved appearance of the soil, and the abundance of feed in the vicinity, satisfied us as to the permanency

6

of the water and the value of the discovery. Although
it was so early in the day, and we were anxious to make
a good march, yet we camped here, as it seemed to be
almost a sin to leave such good quarters. The bed of the
creek is loose sand, through which the water freely
permeates; it is, however, sufficiently coarse not to be
boggy, and animals can approach the water without any
difficulty.

Thursday, January 10.—At twenty minutes past five
A.M., we left our camp with a full supply of water, determined to risk no reverses, and to make a good march. I
should mention that last evening we had been nearly
deafened by the noise of the cicadæ, and but for our large
fires should have been kept awake all night by the mosquitoes. A walk of two miles across a well-grassed plain
brought us to a belt of timber, and we soon afterwards
found ourselves pulled up by a large creek, in which the
water was broad and deep. We had to follow up the bank
of the creek in a N.E. direction for nearly a mile before
we could cross, when to our joy we found that it was
flowing; not a muddy stream from the effects of recent
floods, but a small rivulet of pure water, as clear as crystal.
The bed of the river at this place is deep and rather
narrow. The water flows over sand and pebbles, winding
its way between clumps of melaleuca and gum saplings.
After leaving the river, we kept our old course due north,
crossing in a distance of one mile three creeks with gum-
trees on their banks. The soil of the flats through which
they flow is a red loam of fair quality, and well grassed.
Beyond the third creek is a large plain, parts of which are
very stony; and this is bounded towards the east by a low
stony rise, partly composed of decayed and honey-combed
quartz rock *in situ*, and partly of water-worn pebbles and

other alluvial deposits. At about two miles across this plain, we reached the first of a series of small creeks, with deep water-holes. These creeks and holes have the characteristics peculiar to water-courses which are found in flats formed from the alluvial deposits of schistose rocks. The banks are on a level with the surrounding ground, and are irregularly marked by small trees or only by tufts of long grass, which overhang the channel, and frequently hide it from one's view, even when within a few yards. At about five miles from where we crossed the river, we came to the main creek in these flats, Patten's Creek. It flows along at the foot of a stony range, and we had to trace it up nearly a mile in a N.N.E. direction before we could cross it. As it happened, we might almost as well have followed its course up the flat, for at a little more than two miles we came to it again. We recrossed it at a stony place just below a very large water-hole, and then continued our course over extensive plains, not so well grassed as what we had passed before, and very stony in some places. At eight miles from Patten's Creek, we came to another, running from S.W. to S.E. There was plenty of water in it, but it was evidently the result of recent local rains. On the banks was an abundance of good feed, but very little timber.

Friday, January 11.—Started at five A.M., and in the excitement of exploring fine well-watered country, forgot all about the eclipse of the sun, until the reduced temperature and peculiarly gloomy appearance of the sky drew our attention to the matter. It was then too late to remedy the deficiency, so we made a good day's journey, the moderation of the mid-day heat, which was only about 86°, greatly assisting us. The country traversed has the most verdant and cheerful aspect; abundance of feed and water

6—2

everywhere. All the creeks seen to-day have a course more or less to east by south. The land improves in appearance at every mile. A quantity of rain has fallen here and to the south; and some of the flats are suitable for cultivation if the regularity of the seasons will admit.

COOPER'S CREEK TO CARPENTARIA.

Field-book No. 5.   Camp 92 to 98.   Lat. $22\frac{1}{4}°$ to $21\frac{1}{4}°$.
Standish ranges.

Saturday, January 12.—We started at five A.M., and keeping as nearly as possible a due north course, traversed for about eight miles a splendid flat, through which flow several fine well-watered creeks, lined with white gum-trees. We then entered a series of slaty low sandstone ranges, amongst which were some well-grassed [*here occurs a hiatus*] in the main gullies. The more stony portions are, however, covered with porcupine grass, and here and there with mallee. Large ant-hills are very numerous; they vary in height from two feet and a half to four feet. There was a continuous rise perceptible all the way in crossing the ranges; and from the highest portion, which we reached at a distance of about seven miles, we had a pretty good view of the country towards the north. As far as we could see in the distance, and bearing due north, was a large range, having somewhat the outline of a granite mountain. The east end of this range just comes up to the magnetic north; to the left of this, and bearing N.N.W., is a single conical peak, the top of which only is visible. Farther to the west there were some broken ranges, apparently sandstone; to the east of north the tops of very distant and apparently higher ranges were seen, the outline

of which was so indistinct that I can form no idea as to
their character. The intermediate country below us
appeared alternations of fine valleys and stony ranges such
as we had just been crossing. From here a descent of
two miles brought us to a creek having a northern course;
but on tracing it down for about a mile, we found it turn
to the south-east, and join another from the north. We
crossed over to the latter on a north by west course, and
camped on the west bank. It has a broad, sandy channel;
the water-holes are large but not deep; the banks are
bordered with fine white gums, and are in some places
very scrubby. There is abundance of rich green feed
everywhere in the vicinity. We found numerous indications of blacks having been here, but saw nothing of
them. It seems remarkable that where their tracks are so
plentiful we should [have seen] none since we left King's
Creek. I observed that the natives here climb trees like
those on the Murray, &c., in search of some animal corre-
sponding in habits to the opossum, which they get out
of the hollow branches in a similar manner. I have not
yet been able to ascertain what the animal is.

Sunday, January 13.—We did not leave camp this
morning until half-past seven, having delayed for the
purpose of getting the camels' shoes on—a matter in which
we were eminently unsuccessful. We took our breakfast
before starting, for almost the first time since leaving the
depôt. Having crossed the creek, our course was due
north as before, until at about six miles we came in sight
of the range a-head, when we took a north-half-east
direction, for the purpose of clearing the eastern front of
it. We found the ground more sandy than what we had
before crossed, and a great deal of it even more richly
grassed. Camp 93 is situated at the junction of three

sandy creeks, in which there is abundance of water. The sand is loose, and the water permeates freely, so that the latter may be obtained delightfully cool and clear by sinking anywhere in the beds of the creeks.

COOPER'S CREEK TO CARPENTARIA.

Field-book No. 6.   Lat. 21¼° to 20¼°.   Stations 98 to 105.
Upper part of Cloncurry.*

Saturday, January 19.—Started from Camp 98 at half-past five o'clock A.M., and, passing to the north-west of Mount Forbes, across a fine and well-grassed plain, kept at first a north by east direction. At a distance of three miles, the plain became everywhere stony, being scattered over with quartz pebbles ; and a little farther on we came to low quartz ranges, the higher portions of which are covered with porcupine grass, but the valleys are well clothed with a variety of coarse and rank herbage. At about five miles we crossed a creek with a sandy bed, which has been named Green's Creek. There were blacks not far above where we crossed, but we did not disturb them. After crossing the creek, we took a due north course, over very rugged quartz ranges of an auriferous character. Pieces of iron ore, very rich, were scattered in great numbers over some of the hills. On our being about to cross one of the branch creeks in the low range, we surprised some blacks—a man, who, with a young fellow, apparently his son, was upon a tree cutting out something, and a lubra with a picaninny. The two former did not see me until I was nearly close to them,

* Called after Lord Cloncurry's family, who were related to Mr. Burke. Lady Cloncurry, his cousin, had always been particularly kind to him; and in the paper written by him in his last moments, he mentions her name.

and then they were dreadfully frightened. Jumping down from the trees, they started off, shouting what sounded to us very like " Joe, Joe ! " Thus disturbed, the lubra, who was some distance from them, just then caught sight of the camels and the remainder of the party as they came over the hill into the creek, and this tended to hasten their flight over the stones and porcupine grass. Crossing the range at the head of this creek, we came on a gully running north, down which we proceeded, and soon found it open out into a creek at two or three points, in which we found water. On this creek we found the first specimen of a eucalyptus, which has a very different appearance from the members of the gum-tree race. It grows as high as a good-sized gum-tree, but with the branches less spreading ; in shape it much resembles the elm ; the foliage is dark, like that of the lightwood ; the trunk and branches are covered with a grey bark, resembling in outward appearance that of the box-tree. Finding that the creek was trending too much to the eastward, we struck off to the north again, and at a short distance came on a fine creek running about S.S.E. As it was now about time to camp, we travelled it up for about a mile and a half, and came to a fine water-hole in a rocky basin, at which there were lots of birds.

COOPER'S CREEK TO CARPENTARIA.

Field-book No. 7. Lat. 20¼° to 19¼°. Camps 105 to 112.
Middle part of Cloncurry.

Sunday, January 27.—Started from Camp 105, five minutes past two in the morning. We followed along the bends of the creek by moonlight, and found the creek wind about very much, taking on the whole a N.E. course.

At about five miles it changed somewhat its features; from a broad and sandy channel, winding about through gum-tree flats, it assumes the unpropitious appearance of a straight narrow creek, running in a N.N.E. direction between high perpendicular earthy banks. After running between three or four miles in this manner, it took a turn to the west, at which point there is a fine water-hole, and then assumed its original character. Below this, we found water at several places; but it all seemed to be either from surface drainage or from springs in the sand. The land in the vicinity of the creek appears to have received plenty of rain, the vegetation everywhere being green and fresh; but there is no appearance of the creek having flowed in this part of the channel for a considerable period. Palm-trees are numerous, and some bear an abundance of small round dates (nuts) just ripening. These palms give a most picturesque and pleasant appearance to the creek.

Wednesday, January 30.—Started at half-past seven A.M., after several unsuccessful attempts at getting Golah out of the bed of the creek. It was determined to try bringing him down until we could find a place for him to get out at; but after going in this way two or three miles, it was found necessary to leave him behind, as it was almost impossible to get him through some of the water-holes, and had separated King from the party, which was a matter for very serious consideration, when we found blacks hiding in the box-trees close to us.

Field-book No. 8. Camps 112 to 119. Lat. 19¼° to 17° 53'.
Lower part of Cloncurry. Fieldbook No. 9.

Sunday, February, 1861.—Finding the ground in such a state from the heavy falls of rain that the camels could scarcely be got along, it was decided to leave them at Camp 119, and for Mr. Burke and I to proceed towards the sea on foot. After breakfast we accordingly started, taking with us the horse and three days' provisions. Our first difficulty was in crossing Billy's Creek, which we had to do where it enters the river, a few hundred yards below the camp. In getting the horse in here, he got bogged in a quicksand bank so deeply as to be unable to stir, and we only succeeded in extricating him by undermining him on the creek side, and then lunging him into the water. Having got all the things in safety, we continued down the river bank, which bent about from east to west, but kept a general north course. A great deal of the land was so soft and rotten that the horse, with only a saddle and about twenty-five pounds on his back, could scarcely walk over it. At a distance of about five miles, we again had him bogged in crossing a small creek, after which he seemed so weak, that we had great doubts about getting him on. We, however, found some better ground close to the water's edge, where the sandstone rock runs out, and we stuck to it as far as possible. Finding that the river was bending about so much that we were making very little progress in a northerly direction, we struck off due north, and soon came on some table-land where the soil is shallow and gravelly, and clothed with box and swamp gums. Patches of the land were very boggy, but the main portion was sound enough. Beyond this, we came on an open plain, covered with water up to one's ankles. The soil here was a stiff clay, and the surface very uneven, so that between the tufts of grass one was frequently knee-deep in water. The bottom, however, was sound, and no fear of bogging. After floundering through this for several miles, we came to a path formed by the blacks, and there

were distinct signs of a recent migration in a southerly
direction. By making use of this path, we got on much
better, for the ground was well-trodden and hard. At
rather more than a mile, the path entered a forest, through
which flowed a nice water-course; and we had not gone
far before we found places where the blacks had been
camping. The forest was intersected by little pebbly rises
on which they had 'made their fires, and in the sandy
ground adjoining some of the former had been digging
yams,* which seemed to be so numerous that they could
afford to leave lots of them about, probably having only
selected the very best. We were not so particular, but
ate many of those that they had rejected, and found them
very good. About half a mile farther, we came close on
a black fellow, who was coiling by a camp-fire, whilst his
gin and picaninny were yabbering alongside. We stopped
for a short time to take out some of the pistols that were
on the horse, and that they might see us before we were
so near as to frighten them. Just after we stopped, the
black got up to stretch his limbs, and after a few seconds
looked in our direction. It was very amusing to see the
way in which he stared, standing for some time as if he
thought he must be dreaming, and then, having signalled
to the others, they dropped on their haunches and shuffled
off in the quietest manner possible. Near their fire was a
fine hut, the best I have ever seen, built on the same
principle as those at Cooper's Creek, but much larger and
more complete. I should say a dozen blacks might comfortably coil in it together. It is situated at the end of
the forest, towards the north, and looks out on an extensive
marsh, which is at times flooded by the sea-water. Hundreds of wild geese, plover, and pelicans, were enjoying

* The dioscorea of Carpentaria.

themselves in the water-courses on the marsh, all the water
on which was too brackish to be drinkable, except some
holes that are filled by the stream that flows through the
forest. The neighbourhood of this encampment is one
of the prettiest we have seen during the journey. Proceeding on our course across the marsh, we came to a
channel through which the sea-water enters. Here we
passed three blacks, who, as is universally their custom,
pointed out to us, unasked, the best part down. This
assisted us greatly, for the ground we were taking was
very boggy. We moved slowly down, about three miles,
and then camped for the night. The horse Billy being
completely baked, next morning we started at daybreak,
leaving the horse short-hobbled.

CHAPTER X.

The Object of the Expedition accomplished—Messrs. Burke and
Wills prepare to return to Cooper's Creek—Particulars fur-
nished by King—Diary of the Return Journey—Arrival at
Cooper's Creek.

THE incidents related in the preceding field-book
(No. 9) refer to a journey on foot undertaken on the
9th of February, 1861, by Messrs. Burke and Wills,
with the view of reaching, or at least obtaining a
sight of, the open sea. In this, however, they were
disappointed, in consequence of the swampy nature
of the ground near that part of the coast, which rendered their progress extremely tedious and difficult.
They proceeded, however, about fifteen miles down
the Flinders river, keeping as near to its banks as
possible, when, finding that the tide ebbed and flowed
regularly, and that the water was quite salt, they
determined on returning. They had successfully
accomplished the great object of their mission, by
ENTIRELY CROSSING THE AUSTRALIAN CONTINENT FROM
SOUTH TO NORTH.

The reduced state of their provisions rendered it

absolutely necessary that they should return to
Cooper's Creek as soon as possible; and on the 12th
of February, having rejoined King and Gray, who
had been left at Camp 119 in charge of the camels,
all prepared to commence their glad journey "Homeward."

They started on the 13th of February. The
weather was very wet, for it had been raining continually, and the camels were up to their knees in
mud, so that their stages for a considerable time did
not exceed four or five miles a day. This circumstance no doubt interfered with the regularity of the
entries in the diary.

Before returning to the Diary, it may be well to
furnish the following particulars given by the survivor King in his evidence before the Royal Commission.

Immediately after starting, the allowance of provisions became considerably reduced, and the party
were obliged to rely very much on the portulac.
They had at first five camels* and the horse "Billy,"
but were, in the course of their journey, obliged to
kill three camels as well as the horse ; for the
animals became knocked up, and the flesh helped to
save the party from starvation. Two walked and
two rode, so as to spare the camels as much as
possible.

Gray first began to complain, and gradually grew

* The camel "Golah" had been left behind on 30th January.

worse. King was then attacked with pains in the
legs and back, which he attributed to the fatigue
of walking and the short allowance of provisions;
for they were at last reduced to a quarter of a pound
of flour each daily, a little dried camel meat, and
such allowance of portulac as they could gather.
King, however, recovered himself a good deal. Mr.
Burke was ill for a little time, from having eaten
part of a large snake which they had killed; but he
got better. Mr. Wills suffered the least.

Gray ultimately died, about four days before the
party reached the depôt at Cooper's Creek. He had
complained of suffering from dysentery, although
a usual well-known symptom of that disease did not
appear; and this circumstance, joined to his accounts
of himself, as compared with what was felt by the
others, led them to believe that he was shamming.
It was also discovered that he was in the habit of
secretly consuming more than his fair share of
rations, when the sufferings of the whole party from
famine were very great; and for this offence, King
states that Mr. Burke gave him "six or seven slaps
on the ear." But the party were all on good terms
even after this circumstance, and when Gray's illness
became matter of certainty, his companions were as
kind to him as, poor fellows, it was in their power
to be. They buried him as decently as they could;
and it must affect the stoutest heart to know that
the survivors were all so extremely weak, that it

was as much as they could do to dig his grave: indeed, they were obliged to halt a whole day for that purpose.

When it is added, as will appear hereafter, that the delay of this very day caused additional suffering to the party, and resulted in the loss of the lives of both Messrs. Burke and Wills, language becomes too feeble to describe the painful sensations to which the mournful reminiscence gives rise.

JOURNAL OF THE RETURN FROM CARPENTARIA TO COOPER'S CREEK.

(Transcribed by Mr. James Smith.)

Tuesday, February 19, 1861.—Boocha's Camp.

Wednesday, February 20, 1861.—Pleasant Camp 5, R.

Thursday, February 21, 1861.—Recovery Camp 6, R. Between four and five o'clock a heavy thunderstorm broke over us, having given very little warning of its approach. There had been lightning and thunder towards the S.E. and S. ever since noon yesterday.

The rain was incessant and very heavy for an hour and a half, which made the ground so boggy, that the animals could scarcely walk over it. We nevertheless started at ten minutes to seven A.M., and after floundering along for half an hour halted for breakfast. We then moved on again, but soon found that the travelling was too heavy for the camels, so camped for the remainder of the day. In the afternoon the sky cleared a little, and the sun soon dried the ground, considering. Shot a pheasant, and much disappointed at finding him all feathers and claws. This bird nearly resembles a cock pheasant in plumage; but in other respects it bears more the character of the magpie or crow; the feathers are remarkably wiry and coarse.

Friday, February 22, 1861.—Camp 7, R. A fearful thunderstorm in the evening, about eight P.M., E. S. E., moving gradually round to S. The flashes of lightning were so vivid and incessant as to keep up a continual light for short intervals, overpowering even the moonlight. Heavy rain and strong squalls continued for more than an hour, when the storm moved off W.N.W.; the sky remained more or less overcast for the rest of the night, and the following morning was both sultry and oppressive, with the ground so boggy as to be almost impassable.

Saturday, February 23, 1861.—Camp 8, R.   In spite of the difficulties thrown in our way by last night's storm, we crossed the creek. We were shortly afterwards compelled to halt for the day, on a small patch of comparatively dry ground near the river. The day turned out very fine, so that the soil dried rapidly; and we started in the evening to try a trip by moonlight. We were very fortunate in finding sound ground along a billibong, which permitted of our travelling for about five miles up the creek, when we camped for the night. The evening was most oppressively hot and sultry—so much so, that the slightest exertion made one feel as if he were in a state of suffocation. The dampness of the atmosphere prevented any evaporation, and gave one a helpless feeling of lassitude that I have never before experienced to such an extent. All the party complained of the same sensations, and the horses showed distinctly the effect of the evening trip, short as it was. We had scarcely turned in half an hour when it began to rain, some heavy clouds having come up from the eastward, in place of the layer of small *cirro cumuli* that before ornamented the greater portion of the sky. These clouds soon moved on, and we were relieved from the dread of additional mud. After the sky cleared, the atmosphere became rather cooler and less sultry ; so that, with the assistance of a little smoke to keep the mosquitoes off, we managed to pass a tolerable night.

Sunday, February 24, 1861.—Camp 9, R. Comparatively little rain has fallen above the branch creek with the running water. The vegetation, although tolerably fresh, is not so rank as that we have left. The water in the creek is muddy but good, and has been derived merely from the surface drainage of the adjoining plains. The *Melaleneus* continues in this branch creek, which creeps along the foot of the ranges.

Monday, February 25, 1861.—Camp 10, R. There has been very little rain on this portion of the creek since we passed down. There was, however, no water at all then, at this point. At the Tea-tree Spring, a short distance up the creek, we found plenty of water in the sand, but it had a disagreeable taste from the decomposition of leaves and the presence of mineral matter, probably iron. There seems to have been a fair share of rain along here, everything is so very fresh and green ; and there is water in many of the channels we have [crossed].

Tuesday, February 26, 1861.—Caple Tree Camp, 11, R.

Thursday, February 28, 1861.—Reedy Gully, Camp 12, R. Came into the Reedy Gully Camp about midnight on Tuesday the 26th. Remained there throughout the day on Wednesday, starting at two A.M. on Thursday.

Friday, March 1, 1861.—Camp of the Three Crows, 13, R.

Saturday, March 2, 1861.—Salt-bush Camp, 14, R. Found Golah. He looks thin and miserable. Seems to have fretted a great deal, probably at finding himself left behind, and he has been walking up and down the tracks till he has made a regular pathway. Could find no sign of his having been far off it, although there is splendid feed, to which he could have gone. He began to eat as soon as he saw the other camels.

Sunday, March 3, 1861.—Eureka Camp, 15, R. In crossing a creek by moonlight Charley rode over a large snake. He did not touch him, and we thought it was a log until he struck it with the stirrup-iron. We then saw that it was an immense snake, larger than any that I have ever before seen in a wild state. It measured eight feet four inches in length, and seven inches in girth round the belly. It was nearly the same thickness from the head to within twenty inches of the tail, it then tapered rapidly. The weight was 11½ lbs. From the tip of the nose to five inches back the neck was black, both above and behind; throughout the rest of the body the under part was yellow, and the sides and back had irregular brown transverse bars on a yellowish brown ground. I could detect no poisonous fangs, but there were two distinct rows of teeth in each jaw, and two small claws or nails, about three-eighths of an inch long, one on each side of the vent.

Monday, March 4, 1861.—Feasting Camp, 16, R. Shortly after arriving at Camp 16 we could frequently hear distant thunder towards the east, from which quarter the wind was blowing. During the afternoon there were frequent heavy showers, and towards evening it set in to rain steadily, but lightly. This lasted until about eight P.M., when the rain ceased, and the wind got round to W.; the sky, however, remained overcast until late in the night, and then cleared for a short time; the clouds were soon succeeded by a dense fog, or mist, which continued

until morning.   The vapour having then risen occupied
the upper air in the form of light cir-stratus and cumuli
clouds.

Tuesday, March 5, 1861.—Camp 17, R. Started at
two A.M. on a S.S.W. course, but had soon to turn in on
the creek, as Mr. Burke felt very unwell, having been
attacked by dysentery since eating the snake. He now felt
giddy, and unable to keep his seat. At six A.M., Mr
Burke feeling better, we started again, following along the
creek, in which there was considerably more water than
when we passed down. We camped at 2.15 P.M., at a part
of the creek where the date-trees* were very numerous,
and found the fruit nearly ripe, and very much improved
on what it was when we were here before.

Wednesday, March 6, 1861.—Camp 18, R. Arrived
at the former camp, and find the feed richer than ever, and
the ants just as troublesome. Mr. Burke is a little better,
and Charley looks comparatively well. The dryness of
the atmosphere seems to have a beneficial effect on all.
We found, yesterday, that it was a hopeless matter about
Golah, and we were obliged to leave him behind, as he
seemed to be completely done up, and could not come on,
even when the pack and saddle were taken off.

Thursday, March 7, 1861.—Big-tree Camp, 19, R.
Palm-tree Camp, No. 104, and 20° latitude, by observation
coming down, 20° 21·40'. There is less water here than
there was when we passed down, although there is evidence
of the creek having been visited by considerable floods
during the interval. Feed is abundant, and the vegetation
more fresh than before. Mr. Burke almost recovered, but
Charley is again very unwell, and unfit to do anything.

* Probably *Livistoras.*

7 — 2

He caught cold last night through carelessness in covering himself.

Friday, March 8, 1861.—Camp 20, R. Followed the creek more closely coming up than going down. Found more water in it generally.

Saturday, March 9, 1861.—Camp 21, R. Reached our former camp at 1.30 P.M. Found the herbage much dried up, but still plenty of feed for the camels.

Sunday, March 10, 1861.—Camp 22, R. Camped at the junction of a small creek from the westward, a short distance below our former camp, there being plenty of good water here; whereas the supply at Specimen Camp is very doubtful.

Monday, March 11, 1861.—Camp 23, R. Halted for breakfast at the Specimen Camp at 7.15 A.M. Found more water and feed there than before. Then proceeded up the creek, and got safely over the most dangerous part of our journey. Camped near the head of the gap, in a flat about two miles below our former camp at the gap.

Tuesday, March 12, 1861.—Camp 24, R.

Wednesday, March 13, 1861.—Camp 25, R. Rain all day, so heavily that I was obliged to put my watch and field-book in the pack, to keep them dry. In the afternoon the rain increased, and all the creeks became flooded. We took shelter under some fallen rocks, near which was some feed for the camels; but the latter was of no value, for we had soon to remove them up amongst the rocks, out of the way of the flood, which fortunately did not rise high enough to drive us out of the cave: but we were obliged to shift our packs to the upper part. In the evening the water fell as rapidly as it had risen, leaving everything in a very boggy state. There were frequent light showers during the night.

Thursday, March 14, 1861.—Camp 26, R. Sandstone Cave. The water in the creek having fallen sufficiently low, we crossed over from the cave, and proceeded down the creek. Our progress was slow, as it was necessary to keep on the stony ridge instead of following the flats, the latter being very boggy after the rain. Thinking that the creek must join Scratchley's, near our old camp, we followed it a long way, until, finding it trend altogether too much eastward, we tried to shape across for the other creek, but were unable to do so from the boggy nature of the intervening plain.

Friday, March 15, 1861.—Camp 27, R.

Saturday, March 16, 1861.—Camp 28, R. Scratchley's Creek.

Sunday, March 17, 1861.—Camp 29, R.

Monday, March 18, 1861.—Camp 30, R.

Tuesday, March 19, 1861.—Camp 31, R.

Wednesday, March 20, 1861.—Camp 32, R. Feasting Camp. Last evening the sky was clouded about nine P.M., and a shower came down from the north. At ten o'clock it became so dark that we camped on the bank of the creek, in which was a nice current of clear water. To-day we halted, intending to try a night journey. The packs we overhauled, and left nearly 60lbs. weight of things behind. They were all suspended in a pack from the branches of a shrub close to the creek. We started at a quarter to six, but were continually pulled up by billibongs and branch creeks, and soon had to camp for the night. At the junction of the two creeks just above [are] the three cones, which are three remarkable small hills to the eastward.

Thursday, March 21, 1861.—Humid Camp, 33, R. Unable to proceed on account of the slippery and boggy

state of the ground. The rain has fallen very heavily here
to-day, and every little depression in the ground is either
full of water or covered with slimy mud. Another heavy
storm passed over during the night, almost [extinguishing]
the miserable fire we were able to get up with our very
limited quantity of water-logged and green wood. Having
been so unfortunate last night, we took an early breakfast
this morning at Camp 33, which I have named the Humid
Camp, from the state of dampness in which we found
everything there, and crossing to the east bank of the main
creek, proceeded in a southerly direction nearly parallel
with the creek. Some of the flats near the creek contain
the richest alluvial soil, and are clothed with luxuriant
vegetation. There is an immense extent of plain back, of
the finest character for pastoral purposes, and the country
bears every appearance of being permanently well watered.
We halted on a large billibong at noon, and were favoured
during dinner by a thunderstorm, the heavier portion of
which missed us, some passing north and some south,
which was fortunate, as it would otherwise have spoiled
our baking process, a matter of some importance just now.
We started again at seven o'clock, but the effects of the
heavy rain prevented our making a good journey.

Friday, March 22, 1861.—Muddy Camp, 34, R. Had
an early breakfast this morning, and started before sunrise.
Found that the wet swampy ground that checked our
progress last night was only a narrow strip, and that had
we gone a little farther we might have made a fine journey.
The country consisted of open, well-grassed, pebbly plains,
intersected by numerous small channels, all containing
water. Abundance of fine rich *portulaca* was just bursting
into flower along all these channels, as well as on the
greater portion of the plain. The creek that we camped

on last night ran nearly parallel with us throughout this stage. We should have crossed it to avoid the stony plains, but were prevented by the flood from so doing.

Saturday, March 23, 1861.—Mosquito Camp, 35, R. Started at a quarter to six, and followed down the creek, which has much of the characteristic appearance of the River Burke, where we crossed it on our up journey. The land in the vicinity greatly improves as one goes down, becoming less stony and better grassed. At eleven o'clock we crossed a small tributary from the eastward, and there was a distant range of considerable extent visible in that direction. Halted for the afternoon in a bend, where there was tolerable feed, for the banks are everywhere more or less scrubby.

Sunday, March 24, 1861.—Three-hour Camp, 36, R.

Monday, March 25, 1861.—Native Dog Camp, 37, R. Started at half-past five, looking for a good place to halt for the day. This we found at a short distance down the creek, and immediately discovered that it was close to Camp 89 of our up journey. Had not expected that we were so much to the westward. After breakfast, took some time altitudes, and was about to go back to last camp for some things that had been left, when I found Gray behind a tree, eating skilligolee. He explained that he was suffering from dysentery, and had taken the flour without leave. Sent him to report himself to Mr. Burke, and went on. He having got King to tell Mr. Burke for him, was called up, and received a good thrashing. There is no knowing to what extent he has been robbing us. Many things have been found to run unaccountably short. Started at seven o'clock, the camels in first-rate spirits. We followed our old course back (S.) The first portion of the plains had much the same appearance as when we came up; but that near Camp 88, which then looked so fresh and green, is now very much dried up, and we saw no signs of water anywhere. In fact there seems to have been little or no rain about here since we passed. Soon after three o'clock we struck the first of several small creeks or billibongs, which must be portions of the creek with the deep channel that we crossed on going up, we being now rather to the westward of our former course. From here, after traversing about two miles of the barest clay plain, devoid of all vegetation, we reached a small watercourse, most of the holes in which contained some water of a milky or creamy description. Fine salt bush and portulac being abundant in the vicinity, we camped here at 4.30 A.M. When we started in the evening, a strong breeze had already sprung up in the south, which conveyed much of the characteristic feeling of a hot wind. It increased gradually to a force of five and six, but by eleven o'clock had become decidedly cool, and was so chilly towards morning that we found it necessary to throw on our ponchos. A few cir. cum. clouds were coming up from the east when we started, but we left them behind, and nothing was visible during the night but a thin hazy veil. The gale continued throughout the 26th, becoming warmer as the day advanced. In the afternoon it blew furiously, raising a good deal of dust. The temperature of air at four P.M. was ninety-four degrees in the shade. Wind trees all day.

Tuesday, March 26, 1861.—Salt-bush Camp, 38, R.

Wednesday, March 27, 1861.—Camp 39, R.

Thursday, March 28, 1861.—Camp 40, R.

Friday, March 29, 1861.—Camp 41, R. Camels' last feast. Fine green feed at this camp. Plenty of vine and young polygonums on the small billibongs.

Saturday, March 30, 1861.—Camp 42, R. Boocha's Rest. Employed all day in cutting up, jerking and eating Boocha. The day turned out as favourable for us as we could have wished, and a considerable portion of the meat was completely jerked before sunset.

Sunday, March 31, 1861.—Camp 43, R. Mia Mia Camp. Plenty of good dry feed, various shrubs, salt bushes, including cotton bush and some coarse kangaroo grass; water in the hollows on the stony pavement. The neighbouring country chiefly composed of stony rises and sand-ridges.

Monday, April 1, 1861.—Camp 64, R.

Tuesday, April 2, 1861.—Camp 44, R. Thermometer broken.

Wednesday, April 3, 1861.—Camp 45, R. Salt Meat Camp.

Thursday, April 4, 1861.—Camp 46, R. The Plant Camp.

Friday, April 5, 1861.—Camp 47, R. Oil Camp. Earthy and clayey plains, generally sound and tolerably grassed; but in other places, bare salt bush, withered.

Saturday, April 6, 1861.—Wild Duck Camp, 48, R. Earthy flats, cut into innumerable water-courses, [succeeded by] fine open plains, generally very bare, but having in some places patches of fine salt bush. The dead stalks of portulac and mallows show that those plants are very plentiful in some seasons. [Towards noon came on] earthy plains and numerous billibongs.

Sunday, April 7, 1861.—Camp 49, R. Find the water and feed much dried up. Nearly all the water we have met with has a slightly brackish taste of a peculiar kind, somewhat resembling in flavour potassio-tartrate of soda.

Monday, April 8, 1861.—Camp 50, R. Camped a short

distance above Camp 75. The creek here contains more water, and there is a considerable quantity of green grass in its bed; but it is much dried up since we passed before. Halted fifteen minutes to send back for Gray, who gammoned he could not walk. Some good showers must have fallen lately, as we have passed surface water on the plains every day. In the latter portion of to-day's journey the young grass and portulac are springing freshly in the flats and on the sides of the sand-ridges.

Tuesday, April 9, 1861.—Camp 51, R. Camped on the bank of the creek, where there is a regular field of salt bush, as well as some grass in its bed, very acceptable to the horse, who has not had a proper feed for the last week until last night, and is, consequently, nearly knocked up.

Wednesday, April 10, 1861.—Camp 52, R. Remained at Camp 52, R, all day to cut up and jerk the meat of the horse Billy, who was so reduced and knocked up for want of food, that there appeared little chance of his reaching the other side of the desert; and as we were running short of food of every description ourselves, we thought it best to secure his flesh at once. We found it healthy and tender, but without the slightest trace of fat in any portion of the body.

Thursday, April 11, 1861.—Plenty of water in creek down to this point.

Friday, April 12, 1861.—Extensive earthy plains, intersected by numerous water-courses.

Saturday, April 13, 1861.—Small water-courses lined with lakes. Plenty of salt bush and chrysanthemums on either side. Camped on Stony Desert.

[NOTE BY TRANSCRIBER.—Up to this point, as it appears from Mr. Wills's field-book, the expedition never passed a day in which they did not traverse the banks of, or cross, a creek or other watercourse.]

Sunday, April 14, 1861.

Monday, April 15, 1861.—It commenced to rain lightly at five A.M. this morning, and continued raining pretty steadily throughout the day. Owing to the wet and the exertion of crossing the numerous sand-ridges, Linda became knocked up about four o'clock, and we had to halt at a clay-pan amongst the sand-hills. [The party seems to have crossed a creek near a native camp, about ten A.M.]

Tuesday, April 16, 1861.

Wednesday, April 17, 1861.—This morning, about sunrise, Gray died. He had not spoken a word distinctly since his first attack, which was just as we were about to start.

Thursday, April 18, 1861.—[Another creek and native camp were passed.]

Friday, April 19, 1861 —Camped again without water on the sandy bed of the creek, having been followed by a lot of natives who were desirous of our company; but as we preferred camping alone, we were compelled to move on until rather late, in order to get away from them. The night was very cold. A strong breeze was blowing from the south, which made the fire so irregular that, as on the two previous nights, it was impossible to keep up a fair temperature. Our general course throughout the day had been S.S.E.

Saturday, April 20, 1861.

No entry appears under this date, for now the weary travellers strained every nerve to reach their goal; and it may readily be imagined with what excited feelings they looked forward to the welcome hour which was to restore them, happy and exulting, to their home and friends once more. We learn from King that they had had no provisions, except the dried horse-flesh, for fifteen days previously; and on this day they were allowed to eat as much as they chose, not having the remotest shadow of a doubt that the morrow would bring them to a full supply of food and clothing, and to a happy meeting with the companions they had left behind.

On the 21st they pushed on thirty miles. Mr. Burke rode one of the camels, Mr. Wills and King the other. The poor animals, doubtless, did their best, imagining that they too were approaching a land of plenty. Mr. Burke was a little in advance; and it is touching now to read how he often said, " I think I see their tents ahead;" how he called out the names of his men several times, fondly expecting to hear their voices in reply; but not receiving any answer, supposed that they must have merely shifted to some other part of the creek. Alas! on arriving in the evening at the depôt, to their consternation, they found it deserted. On the morning of that very day, the hearts of the men left at Cooper's Creek had yielded to fears for their own safety, and they were *gone !*

CHAPTER XI.

Disappointment and Depression of the Party on finding the Depôt
deserted—Brahé's Journal of his Stay at Cooper's Creek.

IT is not easy to imagine what must have been the
feelings of the explorers. Here they were, just returned from an enterprise of unexampled difficulty
and danger, which they had brought to a successful
termination at the expense of an unheard-of amount
of privation and suffering, only to find themselves
deserted in their greatest need by companions on
whom they had implicitly relied for succour. Such
sudden depression of spirits, reacting on a state of
high hope and exultation, must have had a withering
effect on frames already exhausted by famine, and
travel-worn to the last degree of human endurance.
Their condition may be better imagined than described.

The sufferers themselves say comparatively little
on the subject, but we learn from King that Mr.
Burke was for some time too much excited to do
anything: and well indeed he might be. After looking round in a state of bewildered astonishment at
the forsaken camp, and noticing that some articles

were scattered about which would certainly have been taken away if a mere change of station near the spot had been intended, Mr. Wills noticed that a tree had been marked with the words "DIG. 21st April, 1861 ; " and at once exclaimed, "They have left here to-day!" He immediately set to work with King to open the ground beneath, and found in a box a few inches below the surface a supply of provisions which had been left for them by Brahé, and a bottle containing a note which was speedily handed up to and read aloud by Mr. Burke. It ran as follows:—

Depôt, Cooper's Creek, April 21, 1861.

The depôt party of V.E.E. leaves this camp to-day to return to the "Darling." I intend to go S.E. from Camp 60, to get into our old track near Bulloo. Two of my companions and myself are quite well; the third— Patten—has been unable to walk for the last eighteen days, as his leg has been severely hurt when thrown by one of the horses. No person has been up here from the "Darling."

We have six camels and twelve horses in good working condition.

WILLIAM BRAHÉ.

Now it must be observed that this note did not contain an accurate description of the real state of the depôt party. None of them were *quite* well, neither were the camels and horses in such good working condition as was represented. Had the explorers known this, they would, in all probability, have decided on following Brahé as soon as they could, and if they had done so they would, doubtless, have been saved. But who could cherish the faintest hope of overtaking a party able to push on with all the vigour of health and strength, at the rate of twenty or thirty miles a day, under circumstances like these? The camels were completely done up, for they had been pressed to the utmost that day, and were not able to travel another mile. The explorers themselves were utterly exhausted. King touchingly says: " It was as much as one of them could do to crawl to the side of the creek for a billy of water." They therefore determined, as any men would have done under the circumstances, to refresh themselves for a day or two with the provisions that had been left, and then endeavour to reach the nearest settlement in the best manner they could.

The following entry by Mr. Wills, under date Sunday, 21st April, 1861, is taken from the diary :—

Arrived at the depôt this evening, just in time to find it deserted. A note left in the plant by Brahé communicates the pleasing information that they have started to-day for the Darling; their camels and horses all well and in good condition. We and our camels being just done up, and scarcely able to reach the depôt, have very little chance of overtaking them. Brahé has fortunately left us ample provisions to take us to the bounds of civilization, namely :— Flour, 50 lbs.; rice, 20 lbs.; oatmeal, 60 lbs.; sugar, 60 lbs.; and dried meat, 15 lbs. These provisions, together with a few horse-shoes and nails and some odds and ends, consti-

tute all the articles left, and place us in a very awkward
position in respect to clothing. Our disappointment at
finding the depôt deserted may easily be imagined —
returning in an exhausted state, after four months of the
severest travelling and privation, our legs almost paralyzed,
so that each of us found it a most trying task only to walk
a few yards. Such a leg-bound feeling I never before
experienced, and I hope never shall again. The exertion
required to get up a slight piece of rising ground, even
without any load, induces an indescribable sensation of
pain and helplessness, and the general lassitude makes one
unfit for anything. Poor Gray must have suffered very
much many times when we thought him shamming. It is
most fortunate for us that these symptoms, which so early
affected him, did not come on us until we were reduced to
an exclusively animal diet of such an inferior description
as that offered by the flesh of a worn-out and exhausted
horse. We were not long in getting out the grub that
Brahé had left, and we made a good supper off some oatmeal porridge and sugar. .This, together with the excitement of finding ourselves in such a peculiar and almost
unexpected position, had a wonderful effect in removing
the stiffness from our legs. Whether it is possible that
the vegetables can so have affected us, I know not; but
both Mr. Burke and I remarked a most decided relief and
a strength in the legs greater than we had had for several
days. I am inclined to think that but for the abundance
of portulac that we obtained on the journey, we should
scarcely have returned to Cooper's Creek at all.

As for Brahé, nothing that can be said here can add
to the bitterness of his reflection, that if he had stood
stedfast for only *one* day more, he would have saved

his leader.   Seven hours more, and he would have had the unspeakable pleasure—the enduring honour —of rescuing from suffering and death, and restoring triumphant to their country, the brave men who had trusted him.   But he was wanting in fortitude: he failed in the determination to stand firm in the exercise of his duty, in the face of *all* discouragement.   Had he possessed but a tithe of the endurance and devotion of his chief, pressed though he was by the entreaties of a sick comrade, he would have stood his ground. The beasts he had would have supplied his party with food for many a day : indeed, they were, even then, far from being at the end of their stock of provisions. However, it fell out otherwise.   The man Patten, who had been complaining for some time, had begged hard, as for his life, to be taken back to Menindie, and Brahé—who, as well as the other European, M'Donough, seems to have entertained an idea that Mr. Burke *might* not come back that way—at last yielded.

The following journal, drawn up by himself before the sad results of his conduct became fully known, will show all that Brahé felt able to say in his own defence at the time it was written :—

To the HON. SECRETARY, Exploration Committee, Melbourne.

Melbourne, June 30, 1861.

SIR,—I have the honour to report to you, for the information of the Committee, that on the 16th of December last Mr. Burke gave me charge of the depôt formed by him at Cooper's Creek, and started for Eyre's Creek *en route* for the Gulf of Carpentaria, at 6.40 A.M., on the same day. His party consisted of himself, Mr. Wills, King, and Gray. He took with him six camels and one horse. The party was provided with provisions for twelve weeks. I accompanied the party for a distance of twenty-two miles along the water-course of the creek.

The party remaining at the depôt consisted of myself, Patten, M'Donough, and Dost Mahomed. My instructions, received by word of mouth, were to remain at the depôt three months or longer, if provisions and other circumstances would permit.

I left the party at four o'clock, P.M., on the same day, and returned to the depôt.

On the following day, the 17th December, we commenced cutting timber, for the purpose of erecting a stockade.

December 22.—Natives, about twenty-five in number, approached the camp, but I considered it advisable not to allow them to come near the tents.

December 30.—On several days during the week were annoyed by a number of natives. On Wednesday they succeeded to steal six camel pack-bags which we had washed that morning, and spread out on the turf on the water's edge to dry. The thief, by keeping under shelter of the high bank, escaped unobserved. Noticing the loss only late in the afternoon, I did not think it advisable to go in pursuit.

During the night of Thursday I observed two blacks within one hundred yards of the camp, but, on my shouting to them, they ran off.

On the 23rd finished the stockade, twenty feet by

eighteen feet, and put up Mr. Burke's tent within it. In this tent I kept the ammunition and firearms. From within the stockade we had the other tents and the camels, which were kept tied up at night, under cover of our guns.

December 31.—Observed some blacks stealing stealthily along the banks of the creek, towards the camp, while one of them directed them from behind a big tree. I allowed them to come within twenty paces of the camp, when, suddenly, I called out to them, we, at the same time firing off our guns over their heads. They seemed much frightened, and hardly able to run away. Great numbers of blacks camped near us.

January 6, 1861.—A large number of natives came to the camp, whose demeanour roused my suspicions. Got hold of a young native, and shoved him off, when he fell down. In the afternoon the whole tribe returned, the men armed, some with spears and some with boomerangs; most of them had painted their faces and bodies. I met them at a short distance from the camp, and marking a circle round it, I gave them to understand that they would be fired at if they entered it. On some of them crossing the line, I fired off my gun into the branches of a tree, when they retired, and did not molest us any more.

December 24.—I should like to explore the neighbourhood a little, but cannot safely leave the camp for longer than three or four hours; one of the men looking after the camels the greater part of the day, while the other is away from four to five hours daily, to prevent the horses from straying. I should have mentioned that I had charge of six camels and twelve horses; two of the camels very scabby. Grass is getting very dry and scarce near the camp. We are obliged to hang all our stores on boughs

8—2

of trees, to protect them from the rats, of which we killed about forty every night for some time.

February 26.—I rode up a conical hill, bearing N.W. by N. from the depôt. It is distant about nine miles, and one of a chain of hills running N.E. and S.W. From the top of this hill I saw another range, distant about fifteen or twenty miles, much broken, and considerably higher than the one I was on. The country between the two is stony, like that between the first range and the depôt.

March 1. — Natives less numerous. Looking out anxiously for Mr. Burke's return. One day I took a ride up the creek, which joins Cooper's Creek opposite our camp, coming from E.S.E., following it up about six miles, and found bed and banks thickly timbered with myall. The country in that direction is very stony. From the top of a stony rise I saw a low range, running E. and W., distant about fifteen miles. Blacks passing now and then, offering us nets and fish. We made it a rule never to accept the least thing from them, but made some of them little presents, as left-off clothes.

March 15.—About twenty-five natives, with their families, passed here last night, on their way up the creek, offering nets and fish. They gave me to understand that there would be plenty of water in the creek shortly, and that we might swim on the flat the stockade was on.

April 1. — During the first twenty-four days of March the heat has been greater than might be expected for the season, and especially the nights were intolerably sultry, a great deal more so than the warmest of January. On the 24th there was a sudden change; it began to blow hard; the nights became very cool. On the evening of the 29th we observed lightning in all quarters, and heard thunder in the north. A slight shower of rain fell between eight and nine o'clock P.M., and another on the following morning, not sufficient, however, to lay the dust. The blacks stole a camel pack-saddle from us on the 27th, while I was away from the camp. They carried it about a mile down the creek, where Patten overtook them, and recovered the saddle, but it was torn to pieces.

April 1.—Patten commenced shoeing the horses, lest he might become incapacitated by disease, as he felt very unwell.

April 4.—Patten, after shoeing two horses, was obliged to take to his bed, suffering acute pain, and was not afterwards able to move about.

April 15.—Patten is getting worse. I and M'Donough begin to feel alarming symptoms of the same disease.

April 18.—There is no probability of Mr. Burke returning this way. Patten is in a deplorable state, and desirous of being removed to the Darling to obtain medical assistance, and our provisions will soon be reduced to a quantity insufficient to take us back to the Darling, if the trip should turn out difficult and tedious. Being also sure that I and M'Donough would not much longer escape scurvy, I, after most seriously considering all circumstances, made up my mind to start for the Darling on Sunday next the 21st. The horses have lately got into the habit of straying; missed five of them a few days ago, and found them about fifteen miles from the camp. Last Monday we had a welcome rain for the first time since the 8th December (except some slight showers on the 24th and 25th March). The last three days have been fine and cool, but now it again looks like rain, although the barometer is very high, higher indeed than it has been during our stay here.

April 21.—Left the depôt at ten o'clock A.M., leaving 50lbs.

of flour, 50 lbs. of oatmeal, 50 lbs. of sugar, and 30 lbs. of rice buried near the stockade at the foot of a large tree, and marked the word " Dig " on the tree. I took 150 lbs. of flour, 75 lbs. of sugar, about 70 lbs. of oatmeal, 1 bag of rice, 4 lbs. of tea, and a small quantity of biscuits. Taking into consideration that we would be obliged to travel slowly on account of Patten, and on account of the scarcity of water, which I calculated to have to contend with, and would probably be on the road to the Darling at least six or seven weeks, I considered that I could not take less provisions. Patten was placed on a quiet camel. We travelled very slowly, and halted at five o'clock P.M., having made about fourteen miles.

There can be no doubt that Brahé afterwards, when too late, felt exceedingly sorry for what he had done, and said that had he known the party would have returned the night they did, he would have remained there certainly.* Of course he would. And it would be hard upon him not to take into consideration the trying circumstances of the case in which he stood. Harassed by the earnest pleadings of the dying man, he no doubt intended to act for the best, and if he failed in firmness of character at this trying moment, it would be unfair towards him not to admit that a like misfortune might in a like case have befallen a much better man.

* Royal Commission, Question 1,732.

CHAPTER XII.

The Explorers determine to move towards Mount Hopeless—Reasons
for Mr. Burke's Choice of that Route—Two Camels killed—
Kindness of the Natives—The Supply of Water fails—The Party
are obliged to retrace their Steps—Find the Nardoo Plant, and
resolve to make a last Attempt to reach Mount Hopeless—Mr.
Wills's last Visit to Cooper's Creek—Friendly Conduct of
Natives—He reaches Depôt, and deposits Journals, &c.—The
Natives visit Mr. Burke's Gunyah—A Fire breaks out—Mr.
Wills rejoins the party—They are reduced to subsist on Nardoo
—Become gradually more and more exhausted.

THROWN entirely on their own resources, the explorers had now no other course left than to consider
what would probably be the best route to the nearest
settlement. After some discussion, they determined
on moving south-west towards Mount Hopeless, not
far from Mount Searle, one of the South Australian
police stations. In taking this step, they were no
doubt influenced by the suggestion thrown out in the
second paragraph of the Committee's written instructions to Mr. Burke; who, from information previously
received, was under the impression that sufficient
water might be obtained the whole way, and that the
entire distance was little more than 150 miles, or less

than half the distance to Menindie. Nothing, therefore, could apparently be more suitable to the condition of the explorers than the proposed route : but a strange fatality seems to have attended all that related to them from the day of their return to the Creek. Mr. Burke's measures, however, seem to have been dictated throughout by a careful consideration of *actual circumstances,* which reflects the highest honour on his character as a leader during the whole of this gloriously successful, although fatal, expedition.

Their minds once made up, the party, with habitual energy, lost no time in preparing to commence their journey. But before doing so, Mr. Burke wrote and deposited in the *cache* the following letter :—

Depôt No. 2, Cooper's Creek, Camp 65.—The return party from Carpentaria, consisting of myself, Wills, and King (Gray dead), arrived here last night, and found that the depôt party had only started on the same day. We proceed on to-morrow slowly down the creek towards Adelaide by Mount Hopeless, and shall endeavour to follow Gregory's track; but we are very weak. The two camels are done up, and we shall not be able to travel faster than four or five miles a day. Gray died on the road, from exhaustion and fatigue. We have all suffered much from hunger. The provisions left here will, I think, restore our strength. We have discovered a practicable route to Carpentaria, the chief portion of which lies on the 140° of E. long. There is some good country between this and the Stony Desert. From there to the tropics the country is dry and stony. Between the tropics and Carpentaria a considerable portion is rangy, but is well watered and richly grassed. We reached the shores of Carpentaria on the 11th of February, 1861. Greatly disappointed at finding the party here gone.

(Signed) ROBERT O'HARA BURKE,
Leader.

April 22, 1861.

P.S.—The camels cannot travel, and we cannot walk, or we should follow the other party. We shall move very slowly down the creek.

They then covered up the *cache,* so as to leave it as nearly as possible in the condition in which they found it, believing that the word " DIG," already cut on the tree, would answer their purpose as well as it had answered Brahé's; for they had no reason to think it possible that Brahé himself would return to the depôt so soon, as afterwards turned out to be the case. Their supply of provisions was, considering everything, tolerably good, and might be fairly calculated to last at least a month, so that, with the assistance of the two camels, they had every reason to believe they might easily reach Mount Hopeless in sufficient time to preserve their lives, and reap the reward of their successful exertions.

The party started at a quarter past nine o'clock on the morning of Thursday, the 23rd of April, 1861, the second day after their return to Cooper's Creek.

The following diary gives full particulars of their wanderings, and of the heroism, patience, and mutual

fidelity with which the suffering party performed
their duty to the last. The melancholy story, as
related by Mr. Wills, will (with one trifling exception,* caused by the disturbed state of mind of the
narrator) be found to agree with the narrative furnished by the sole survivor, John King. This narrative will be found entire in the appendix, but full
extracts from it will also be inserted whenever it
becomes necessary to supply missing links in the
chain of the story.

JOURNAL OF TRIP FROM COOPER'S CREEK TOWARDS ADELAIDE,
APRIL, 1861.

(Transcribed by Mr. Archer.)

The advance party of the Victorian Exploring Expedition, consisting of Burke, Wills, and King (Gray being
dead), having returned from Carpentaria on the 21st April
in an exhausted and weak state, and finding that the depôt
party left at Cooper's Creek had started for the Darling,
with their horses and camels fresh and in good condition,
deemed it useless to attempt to overtake them, having only
two camels, both done up, and being so weak themselves
as to be unable to walk more than four or five miles a
day; finding also that the provisions left at the depôt for
them would scarcely take them to Menindie, started down
Cooper's Creek for Adelaide viâ Mount Hopeless, on the
morning of the 23rd April, intending to follow as nearly as
possible the route taken by Gregory; by so doing they
hope to be able to recruit themselves and the camels,
whilst ·sauntering slowly down the creek, and to have

* The number of days during which they rested at Cooper's Creek.

sufficient provisions left to take them comfortably, or at least without risk, to some station in South Australia. Their equipment consists of the following articles:—Flour, 50 lbs.; sugar, 60 lbs.; rice, 20 lbs.; oatmeal, 60 lbs.; jerked meat, 25 lbs.; ginger, 2 lbs.; salt, 1 lb.

Tuesday, April 23. From Depôt.—Having collected together all the odds and ends that seemed likely to be of use to us, in addition to the provisions left in the plant, we started at a quarter past nine A.M., keeping down the southern bank of the creek. We only went about five miles, and camped at half-past eleven on a billibong, where the feed was pretty good. We find the change of diet already making a great improvement in our spirits and strength. The weather is delightful, days agreeably warm, but the nights very chilly. The latter is more noticeable from our deficiency in clothing, the depôt party having taken all the reserve things back with them to the Darling. To Camp 1.

Wednesday April 24. From Camp 1.—As we were about to start this morning, some blacks came by, from whom we were fortunate enough to get about twelve pounds of fish for a few pieces of straps and some matches, &c. This is a great treat for us, as well as a valuable addition to our rations. We started at a quarter past eight P.M., on our way down to the creek, the blacks going in the opposite direction, little thinking that in a few miles they would be able to get lots of pieces for nothing, better than those they had obtained from us. To Camp 2.

Thursday, April 25. From Camp 2.—Awoke at five o'clock, after a most refreshing night's rest. The sky was beautifully clear and the air rather chilly. The terrestrial radiation seems to have been considerable, and a slight

dew had fallen.   We had scarcely finished breakfast when
our friends the blacks, from whom we obtained the fish,
made their appearance with a few more, and seemed inclined to go with us and keep up the supply.   We gave
them some sugar, with which they were greatly pleased.
They are by far the most well-behaved blacks we have
seen on Cooper's Creek.   We did not get away from the
camp until half-past nine A.M., continuing our course down
the most southern branch of the creek, which keeps a
general S.W. course.   We passed across the stony point
which abuts on one of the largest water-holes in the
creek, and camped at half-past twelve about a mile
below the most dangerous part of the rocky path.   At this
latter place we had an accident that might have resulted
badly for us.   One of the camels fell while crossing the
worst part, but we fortunately got him out with only a few
cuts and bruises.   The water-hole at this camp is a very
fine one, being (to Camp 3) several miles long, and on an
average about   * chains broad.   The waterfowl are numerous, but rather shy—not nearly so much so, however,
as those on the creeks between here and Carpentaria, and I
am convinced that the shyness of the latter, which was
also remarked by Sturt on his trip to Eyre's Creek, arises
entirely from the scarcity of animals, both human and
otherwise, and not from any peculiar mode of catching
them that the blacks may have.

Friday, April 26.   *From Camp* 3.—Last night was
beautifully calm, and comparatively warm, although the
sky was very clear.   Reloaded the camels by moonlight
this morning, and started at a quarter to six.   Striking off
to the south of the creek, we soon got on a native path,
which leaves the creek just below the stony ground, and

* *Sic.*

takes a course nearly west across a piece of open country, bounded on the south by sand-ridges, and on the north by the scrubby ground which flanks the bank of the creek at this part of its course.   Leaving the path on the right at a distance of three miles, we turned up a small creek which passes down between some sand-hills; and finding a nice patch of feed for the camels at a water-hole, we halted at fifteen minutes past seven for breakfast.   We started again at fifty minutes past nine A.M.   Continuing our westerly course along the path, we crossed to the south of the water-course above the water, and proceeded over the most splendid salt-bush country that one could wish to see, bounded on the left by sand-hills, whilst to the right the peculiar looking flat-topped sandstone ranges form an extensive amphitheatre, through the far side of the arena of which may be traced the dark line of creek timber.   At twelve o'clock we camped in the bed of the creek, at Camp ,* our last camp on the road down from the Gulf, having taken four days to do what we then did in one.   This comparative rest, and the change in diet, have also worked wonders, however; the leg-tied feeling is now entirely gone, and I believe that in less than a week we shall be fit to undergo any fatigue whatever.   The camels are improving, and seem capable of doing all that we are likely to require of them.   To Camp 4.

Saturday, April 27.—First part of the night clear, with a light breeze from the S.   Temperature at midnight 10° (Reaumur); towards morning there were a few cir. cum. clouds passing over N.E. to S.W., but these disappeared before daylight; at five A.M. the temperature was 7·5° (Reaumur).   We started at six o'clock, and, following the native path, which at about a mile from our camp takes a

* *Sic.*

southerly direction, we soon came to the high sandy alluvial deposit, which separates the creek at this point from the stony rises.   Here we struck off from the path, keeping well to the south of the creek, in order that we might mess in a branch of it that took a southerly direction.   At twenty minutes past nine we came in on the creek again where it runs due south, and halted for breakfast at a fine water-hole, with fine fresh feed for the camels.   Here we remained until noon, when we moved on again, and camped at one o'clock on a general course, having been throughout the morning S.W. eight miles.   The weather is most agreeable and pleasant; nothing could be more favourable to us up to the present time.   The temperature in the shade at half-past ten A.M. was 17·5 (Reaumur), with a light breeze from south, and a few small cir. cum. clouds towards the north.   I greatly feel the want of more instruments, the only things I have left being my watch, prism, compass, pocket compass, and one thermometer (Reaumur). To Camp 5.

Sunday, April 28. *From Camp* 5.—Morning fine and calm, but rather chilly.   Started at a quarter to five A.M., following down the bed of a creek in a westerly direction, by moonlight.   Our stage was, however, very short, for about a mile one of the camels (Linda) got bogged by the side of a water-hole, and although we tried every means in our power, we found it impossible to get him out.   All the ground beneath the surface was a bottomless quicksand, through which the beast sank too rapidly for us to get bushes or timber fairly beneath him, and being of a very sluggish, stupid nature, he could never be got to make sufficiently strenuous efforts towards extricating himself.   In the evening, as a last chance, we let the water in from the creek, so as to buoy him up and at the same time soften the ground about his legs, but it was of no avail.   The brute lay quietly in it as if he quite enjoyed his position.   To Camp 6.

Monday, April 29.   *From Camp* 6.—Finding Linda still in the hole, we made a few attempts to extricate him, and then shot him, and after breakfast commenced cutting off what flesh we could get at for jerking.

Tuesday, April 30.   *Camp* 6.—Remained here to-day for the purpose of drying the meat, for which process the weather is not very favourable.

Wednesday, May 1.   *From Camp* 6.—Started at twenty minutes to nine, having loaded our only camel, Rajah, with the most necessary and useful articles, and packed up a small swag each of bedding and clothing for our own shoulders.   We kept on the right bank of the creek for about a mile, and then crossed over at a native camp to the left, where we got on a path running due W., the creek having turned to the N.   Following the path, we crossed an open plain, and then sand-ridges, whence we saw the creek straight ahead of us, running nearly S. again. The path took us to the southernmost point of the bend, in a distance of about two and a half miles from where we had crossed the creek, thereby saving us from three to four miles, as it cannot be less than six miles round by the creek.   To Camp 7.

Thursday, May 2.   *Camp* 7.—Breakfasted by moonlight, and started at half-past six.   Following down the left bank of the creek in a westerly direction, we came, at a distance of six miles, on a lot of natives, who were camped on the bed of a creek.   They seemed to have just breakfasted, and were most liberal in their presentations of fish and cake.   We could only return the compliment by some fish-hooks and sugar.   About a mile further on we came

to a separation of the creek, where what looked like the
main branch looked towards the south.   This channel we
followed, not, however, without some misgivings as to its
character, which were soon increased by the small and un-
favourable appearance that the creek assumed.   On our
continuing along it a little farther it began to improve, and
widened out with fine water-holes of considerable depth.
The banks were very steep, and a belt of scrub lined it on
either side.   This made it very inconvenient for travelling,
especially as the bed of the creek was full of water for a
considerable distance.   At eleven A.M. we halted until
half-past one P.M., and then moved on again, taking a
S.S.W. course for about two miles, when, at the end of a
very long water-hole, it breaks into billibongs, which continue splitting into sandy channels until they are all lost in
the earthy soil of a box forest.   Seeing little chance of
water a-head, we turned back to the end of the long water-
hole, and camped for the night.   On our way back Rajah
showed signs of being done up.   He had been trembling
greatly all the morning.*   On this account his load was
further lightened to the amount of a few pounds, by doing
away with the sugar, ginger, tea, cocoa, and two or three
tin plates.   To Camp No. 8.

  Friday, May 3. *Camp* 8.—Started at seven A.M.,
striking off in a northerly direction for the main creek.
At a mile and a half came to a branch which (left un-
finished.)   To Camp No. 9.

  Saturday, May 4. *Junction from Camp* 9.—Night and

---

* The poor brute, no doubt, fretted for his dead companion Linda.
It will be remembered that one of the camels (Golah), previously lost
on the trip to Carpentaria, was found on the 2nd March, looking thin
and miserable, with evident tokens of not having fed for a considerable time ; but when he saw the other camels he began to eat.

morning very cold. Sky clear, almost calm; occasionally a light breath of air from south. Rajah appears to feel the cold very much. He was so stiff this morning as to be scarcely able to get up with his load. Started to return down the creek at 6.45, and halted for breakfast at nine A.M., at the same spot as we breakfasted at yesterday. Proceeding from there down the creek, we soon found a repetition of the features that were exhibited by the creek examined on Thursday. At a mile and a half we came to the last water-hole, and below that the channel became more sandy and shallow, and continued to send off billibongs to the south and west, slightly changing its course each time until it disappeared altogether in a north-westerly direction. Leaving King with the camel, we went on a mile or two to see if we could find water, and being unsuccessful, we were obliged to return to where we had breakfasted, as being the best place for feed and water.

Sunday, May 5.—To Camp 10.—Started by myself to reconnoitre the country in a southerly direction, leaving Mr. Burke and King with the camel at Camp No. 10. Travelled S. W. by S. for two hours, following the course of the most southerly billibongs. Found the earthy soil becoming more loose and cracked up, and the box-track gradually disappearing. Changed course to west for a high sand-ridge, which I reached in one hour and a half, and continuing in the same direction to one still higher, obtained from it a good view of the surrounding country. To the north were the extensive box forests bounding the creek on either side. To the east earthy plains intersected by water-courses and lines of timber, and bounded in the distance by sand-ridges. To the south the projection of the sand-ridge partially intercepted the view; the rest was composed of earthy plains, apparently clothed with chry-

9

santhemums. To the westward, another but smaller plain was bounded also by high sand-ridges, running parallel with the one on which I was standing. This dreary prospect offering no encouragement for one to proceed, I returned to Camp 10, by a more direct and better route than I had come, passing over some good salt-bush land which borders on the billibongs to the westward.

Monday, May 6.—From Camp 10 back to Camp 9. Moved up the creek again to Camp 9 at the junction, to breakfast, and remained the day there. The present state of things is not calculated to raise our spirits much. The rations are rapidly diminishing; our clothing, especially the boots, are all going to pieces, and we have not the materials for repairing them properly; the camel is completely done up, and can scarcely get along, although he has the best of feed, and is resting half his time. I suppose this will end in our having to live like the blacks for a few months.

Tuesday, May 7.—*Camp* 9.—Breakfasted at daylight, but when about to start, found that the camel would not rise, even without any load on his back. After making every attempt to get him up, we were obliged to leave him to himself. Mr. Burke and I started down the creek to reconnoitre. At about eleven miles we came to some blacks fishing. They gave us some half a dozen fish each for luncheon, and intimated that if we would go to their camp we should have some more, and some bread. I tore in two a piece of macintosh stuff that I had, and Mr. Burke gave one piece, and I the other. We then went on to their camp, about three miles farther. They had caught a considerable quantity of fish, but most of them were small. I noticed three different kinds—a small one that they call cupi, five to six inches long, and

not broader than an eel; the common one, with large
coarse scales, termed peru ; and a delicious fish, some of
which run from a pound to two pounds weight.   The
natives call them cawilchi.   On our arrival at the camp, .
they led us to a spot to camp on, and soon afterwards
brought a lot of fish and bread, which they call nardoo.
The lighting a fire with matches delights them, but they
do not care about having them.   In the evening various
members of the tribe came down with lumps of nardoo
and handfuls of fish, until we were positively unable
to eat any more.   They also gave us some stuff they
call bedgery, or pedgery.   It has a highly intoxicating
effect when chewed even in small quantities.   It appears
to be the dried stems and leaves of some shrub.

Wednesday, May 8.—Left the blacks' camp at half-past
seven, Mr. Burke returning to the junction, whilst I proceeded to trace down the creek.   This I found a shorter
task than I had expected, for it soon showed signs of
running out, and at the same time kept considerably to the
north of west.   There were several fine water-holes within
about four miles of the camp I had left, but not a drop
all the way beyond that, a distance of seven miles.   Finding that the creek turned greatly towards the north, I
returned to the blacks' encampment ; and, as I was about
to pass, they invited me to stay.   So I did so, and was
even more hospitably entertained than before, being on
this occasion offered a share of a gunyah, and supplied
with plenty of fish and nardoo, as well as a couple of
nice fat rats.   The latter found most delicious.   They
were baked in the skins.   Last night was clear and calm,
but unusually warm.   We slept by a fire just in front of
the blacks' camp.   They were very attentive in bringing
us firewood, and keeping fire up during the night.

9—2

Thursday, May 9.—Parted from my friends the blacks at half-past seven, and started for Camp 9.

Friday, May 10.—Camp 9.—Mr. Burke and King employed in jerking the camel's flesh,* whilst I went out to look for the nardoo seed for making bread. In this I was unsuccessful, not being able to find a single tree of it in the neighbourhood of the camp. I however tried boiling the large kind of bean which the blacks call padlu; they boil easily, and when shelled are very sweet, much resembling in taste the French chestnut. They are to be found in large quantities nearly everywhere.

Saturday, May 11.—Camp 9.—To-day Mr. Burke and King started down the creek for the blacks' camp, determined to ascertain all particulars about the nardoo seed. I have now my turn at the meat jerking, and must devise some means for trapping the birds and rats, which is a pleasant prospect after our dashing trip to Carpentaria, having to hang about Cooper's Creek living like the blacks.

Sunday, May 12.—Mr. Burke and King returned this morning, having been unsuccessful in their search for the blacks, who, it seems, have moved over to the other branch of the creek. Decided on moving out on the main creek to-morrow, and then trying to find the natives of the creek.

Monday, May 13.—Shifted some of the things and brought them back again, Mr. Burke thinking it better for one to remain here with them for a few days, so as to eat the remains of the fresh meat, whilst the others went in search of the blacks and nardoo.

Tuesday, May 14.—Mr. Burke and King gone up the

* Their last camel (Rajah) was shot this day, as the poor brute was evidently on the point of dying. *Vide* King's Narrative.

creek to look for blacks, with four days' provisions. Self
employed in preparing for a final start on their return.
This evening Mr. Burke and King returned, having been
some considerable distance up the creek, and found no
blacks. It is now settled that we plant the things, and all
start together the day after to-morrow.*   The weather
continues very fine; the nights calm, clear, and cold, and
the days clear, with a breeze generally from S., but to-day
from E., for a change. This makes the first part of the
day rather cold. When clouds appear, they invariably
move from W. to E.

Wednesday, May 15.—*Camp* 9.—Planting the things,
and preparing to leave the creek for Mount Hopeless.

Thursday, May 16.—Having completed our planting,
&c., started up the creek to the second blacks' camp, a
distance of about eight miles. Finding our loads rather
too heavy, we made a small plant here of such articles as
could best be spared.

Friday, May 17.—*Nardoo.*—Started this morning on a
blacks' path, leaving the creek on our left, our intention
being to keep a south-easterly direction until we should
cut some likely-looking creek, and then to follow it down.
On approaching the foot of the first sand-hill, King caught
sight in the flat of some nardoo seeds, and we soon found
that the flat was covered with them. This discovery
caused somewhat of a revolution in our feelings, for we
considered that with the knowledge of this plant we were
in a position to support ourselves, even if we were destined
to remain on the creek and wait for assistance from town.
Crossing some sand-ridges running N. and S., we struck

---

* They had now decided to make a second attempt to reach
Mount Hopeless. At this time the poor sufferers had become
dreadfully wearied, and their daily ration had become much reduced.

into a creek which runs out of Cooper's Creek, and followed it down. At about five miles we came to a large water-hole, beyond which the water-course runs out on extensive flats and earthy plains. Calm night; sky cleared towards morning, and it became very cold. A slight easterly breeze sprang up at sunrise, but soon died away again. The sky again became overcast, and remained so throughout the day. There was occasionally a light breeze from the south, but during the greater portion of the day it was quite calm. Fine halo around the sun in the afternoon.

Saturday, May 18.—*Camp* 16.—(No entry except the following meteorological entry on an opposite page, which may probably refer to this date.) Calm night, sky sometimes clear and sometimes partially overcast with veil clouds.

Sunday, May 19.—(No entry beyond this citation of date.)

Monday, May 20.—(No entry beyond this.)

Tuesday, May 21.—*Creek.*—(No entry beyond this.)

Wednesday, May 22. — *Cooper's Creek.* — (No entry beyond this.)

Thursday, May 23.—(No entry beyond this.)

Friday, May 24.—Started with King to celebrate the Queen's birthday, by fetching from Nardoo Creek what is now to us the staff of life. Returned at a little after two P.M., with a fair supply, but find the collecting of the seed a slower and more troublesome process than could be desired. Whilst picking the seed, about eleven o'clock A.M., both of us heard distinctly the noise of an explosion, as of a gun, at some considerable distance. We supposed it to have been a shot fired by Mr. Burke; but on returning to the camp, found that he had not fired

nor heard the noise.   The sky was partially overcast with
high cum. str. clouds, and a light breeze blew from the east,
but nothing to indicate a thunderstorm in any direction.

The following extract from King's narrative refers
to the period :—

Mr. Wills and I went out to gather nardoo, of which we
obtained a supply sufficient for three days ; and finding
a pounding-stone at the gunyahs, Mr. Burke and I pounded
the seed, which was such slow work that we were compelled to use half flour and half nardoo.   Mr. Burke and
Mr. Wills then went down the creek for the remainder of
the dried meat which we had planted, and we had now all
our things with us, gathering nardoo, and living the best
way we could.   Mr. Burke requested Mr. Wills to go up
the creek as far as the depôt, and to place a note in the
plant there, stating that we were then living on the creek,
the former note having stated that we were on our road to
South Australia.*   He also was to bury there the field-
books of the journey to the Gulf.   Before starting he got
3 lbs. of flour and 4 lbs. of pounded nardoo, and about a
pound of meat, as he expected to be absent about eight
days.   During his absence, I gathered nardoo and pounded
it, as Mr. Burke wished to lay in a supply in case of rain.

Diary continued :—

Monday, May 27.—Started up the creek this morning
for the depôt, in order to deposit journals and a record of
the state of affairs here.   On reaching the sand-hills below
where Linda was bogged, I passed some blacks on a flat
collecting nardoo seed.   Never saw such an abundance of

* As far as Mr. Burke was concerned, he does not seem to have
omitted a single thing necessary for the safety of his party.

the seed before. The ground in some parts was quite
black with it. There were only two or three gins and
children, and they directed me on, as if to their camp, in
the direction I was before going; but I had not gone far
over the first sand-hill when I was overtaken by about
twenty blacks, bent on taking me back to their camp,
and promising any quantity of nardoo and fish. On my
going with them, one carried the shovel, and another
insisted on taking my swag, in such a friendly manner
that I could not refuse them. They were greatly amused
with the various little things I had with me. In the
evening they supplied me with abundance of nardoo and
fish; and one of the old men, Poko Tinnamira, shared his
gunyah with me. . . . The night was very cold, but,
by the help of several fires—[The entry suddenly stops,
but in the margin of the opposite page are written the
names of several natives and certain native words, with
their meanings in English.]

Tuesday, May 28.—Left the blacks' camp, and proceeded
up the creek. Obtained some mussels near where Linda
died, and halted for breakfast. Still feel very unwell from
the effects of the constipation of the bowels. After breakfast, travelled on to our third camp coming down.

Wednesday, May 29.—Started at seven o'clock, and
went on to the duck-holes, where we breakfasted coming
down. Halted there at thirty minutes past nine for a feed,
and then moved on. At the stones saw a lot of crows
quarrelling about something near the water. Found it to
be a large fish, of which they had eaten a considerable
portion. Finding it quite fresh and good, I decided the
quarrel by taking it with me. It proved a most valuable
addition to my otherwise scanty supper of nardoo porridge.
This evening I camped very comfortably in a Mia Mia,

about eleven miles from the depôt. The night was very cold, although not entirely cloudless. A brisk easterly breeze sprang up in the morning, and blew freshly all day. In the evening the sky clouded in, and there were one or two slight showers, but nothing to wet the ground.

Thursday, May 30.—Reached the depôt this morning, at eleven o'clock. No traces of any one except blacks having been here since we left. Deposited some journals, and a notice of our present condition. Started back in the afternoon, and camped at the first water-hole. Last night being cloudy, was unusually warm and pleasant.

Mr. Wills's last letter :—

Depôt Camp, May 30.

We have been unable to leave the creek. Both camels are dead, and our provisions are done. Mr. Burke and King are down the lower part of the creek. I am about to return to them, when we shall probably come up this way. We are trying to live the best way we can, like the blacks, but find it hard work. Our clothes are going to pieces fast. Send provisions and clothes as soon as possible.

W. J. Wills.

The depôt party having left, contrary to instructions, has put us in this fix. I have deposited some of my journals here, for fear of accidents.

(Signed) W. J. W.

Friday, May 31.—Decamped at thirty minutes past seven, having first breakfasted. Passed between the sand-hills at nine, and reached the blanket Mia Mias at twenty minutes to eleven ; from there proceeded on to the rocks, where I arrived at half-past one, having delayed about half an hour on the road in gathering some portulac. It had been a fine morning, but the sky now became over-

cast, and threatened to set in for a steady rain; and as I
felt very weak and tired I only moved on about a mile
farther, and camped in a sheltered gully, under some
bushes. Night clear and very cold. No wind. Towards
morning sky became slightly overcast with cirro str.
clouds.

Saturday, June 1.—Started at a quarter to eight A.M.
Passed the duck-holes at ten A.M., and my second camp
up at two P.M., having rested in the meantime about forty-
five minutes. Thought to have reached the blacks' camp,
or at least where Linda was bogged, but found myself
altogether too weak and exhausted; in fact, had extreme
difficulty in getting across the numerous little gullies,
and was at last obliged to camp, from sheer fatigue.
Night ultimately clear and cloudy, with occasional
showers.

Sunday, June 2.—Started at half-past six, thinking to
breakfast at the blacks' camp, below Landa's grave; found
myself very much fagged, and did not arrive at their camp
until ten A.M., and then found myself disappointed as to a
good breakfast, the camp being deserted. Having rested
awhile, and eaten a few fish-bones, I moved down the
creek, hoping by a late march to be able to reach our
own camp, but I soon found, from my extreme weakness,
that that would be out of the question. A certain amount
of good luck, however, still stuck to me, for, on going
along by a large water-hole, I was so fortunate as to find
a large fish, about a pound and a-half in weight, which
was just being choked by another which it had tried to
swallow, but which had stuck in its throat. I soon had a
fire lit, and both of the fish cooked and eaten. The large
one was in good condition. Moving on again after my
late breakfast, I passed Camp 67 of the journey to Car-

pentaria, and camped for the night under some polygonum bushes.

Monday, June 3.—Started at seven o'clock, and, keeping on the south bank of the creek, was rather encouraged, at about three miles, by the sound of numerous crows a-head; presently fancied I could see smoke, and was shortly afterwards set at my ease by hearing a cooey from Pitchery, who stood on the opposite bank, and directed me around the lower end of the water-hole, continually repeating his assurance of abundance of fish and bread. Having with some considerable difficulty managed to ascend the sandy path that led to the camp, I was conducted by the chief to a fire, where a large pile of fish were just being cooked in the most approved style. These I imagined to be for the general consumption of the half a dozen natives gathered around, but it turned out that they had already had their breakfast. I was expected to dispose of this lot—a task which, to my own astonishment, I soon accomplished, keeping two or three blacks pretty steadily at work extracting bones for me. The fish being disposed of, next came a supply of nardoo cake and water, until I was so full as to be unable to eat any more; when Pitchery, allowing me a short time to recover myself, fetched a large bowl of the raw nardoo flour, mixed to a thin paste, a most insinuating article, and one that they appear to esteem a great delicacy. I was then invited to stop the night there, but this I declined, and proceeded on my way home.

Tuesday, June 4.—Started for the blacks' camp, intending to test the practicability of living with them, and to see what I could learn as to their ways and manners.

Wednesday, June 5.—Remained with the blacks. Light rain during the greater part of the night, and more or less

throughout the day, in showers. Wind blowing in squalls
from S.*

Thursday, June 6.—Returned to our own camp; found
that Mr. Burke and King had been well supplied with fish
by the blacks. Made preparation for shifting our camp
nearer to theirs on the morrow.

Friday, June 7.—Started in the afternoon for the blacks'

---

* A few days after Mr. Wills left, some natives came down the
creek to fish at some water-holes near our camp. They were very
civil to us at first, and offered us some fish ; on the second day they
came again to fish, and Mr. Burke took down two bags, which they
filled for him ; on the third day they gave us one bag of fish, and
afterwards all came to our camp. We used to keep our ammunition
and other articles in one gunyah, and all three of us live together in
another. One of the natives took an oilcloth out of this gunyah,
and Mr. Burke seeing him run away with it, followed him with his
revolver, and fired over his head ; and upon this the native dropped
the oilcloth. While he was away the other blacks invited me away
to a water-hole, to eat fish ; but I declined to do so, as Mr. Burke
was away, and a number of natives were about who would have
taken all our things. When I refused, one took his boomerang and
laid it over my shoulder, and then told me by signs that if I called
out for Mr. Burke, as I was doing, he would strike me. Upon this
I got them all in front of the gunyah, and fired a revolver over their
heads ; but they did not seem at all afraid, until I got out the gun,
when they all ran away. Mr. Burke, hearing the report, came back,
and we saw no more of them until late that night, when they came
with some cooked fish, and called out "white fellow." Mr. Burke
then went out with his revolver, and found a whole tribe coming
down, all painted, and with fish in small nets, carried by two men.
Mr. Burke went to meet them, and they wished to surround him ;
but he knocked as many of the nets of fish out of their hands as he
could, and shouted out to me to fire. I did so, and they ran off. We
collected five small nets of cooked fish. The reason he would not
accept the fish from them was, that he was afraid of being too
friendly, lest they should be always at our camp. We then lived on
fish until Mr. Wills returned.—*King's Narrative.*

camp, with such things as we could take; found ourselves all very weak, in spite of the abundant supply of fish that we have lately had. I myself could scarcely get along, although carrying the lightest swag, only about 30 lbs. Found that the blacks had decamped, so determined on proceeding to-morrow up to the next camp, near the nardoo field.

Saturday, June 8.—With the greatest fatigue and difficulty we reached the nardoo camp. No blacks, greatly to our disappointment. Took possession of the best Mia Mia, and rested for the remainder of the day.

Sunday, June 9,—King and I proceeded to collect nardoo, leaving Mr. Burke at home.

Monday, June 10.—Mr. Burke and King collecting nardoo; self at home, too weak to go out. Was fortunate enough to shoot a crow.

Tuesday, June 11.—King out for nardoo. Mr. Burke up the creek, to look for the blacks.

Wednesday, June 12.—King out collecting nardoo. Mr. Burke and I at home, pounding and cleaning. I still feel myself, if anything, weaker in the legs, although the nardoo appears to be more thoroughly (?) digested.

Thursday, June 13.—Last night the sky was pretty clear, and the air rather cold, but nearly calm; a few cir.-st. hung about the N.E. horizon during the first part of the night. Mr. Burke and King out for nardoo. Self weaker than ever; scarcely able to go to the water-hole for water. Towards afternoon cir.-cum. and cir.-st. began to appear, moving northward, scarcely any wind all day.

Friday, June 14.—Night alternately clear and cloudy; cir.-cum. and cum.-st. moving northwards; no wind; beautifully mild for the time of year; in the morning, some heavy clouds on the horizon. King out for nardoo;

brought in a good supply. Mr. Burke and I at home, pounding and cleaning seed. I feel weaker than ever, and both Mr. B. and King are beginning to feel very unsteady in the legs.

Saturday, June 15.—Night clear, calm, and cold; morning very fine, with a light breath of air from N.E. King out for nardoo; brought in a fine supply. Mr. Burke and I pounding and cleaning. He finds himself getting very weak, and I am not a bit stronger. I have determined on beginning to chew tobacco and eat less nardoo, in hopes that it may induce some change in the system. I have never yet recovered from constipation, the effect of which is exceedingly painful.

Sunday, June 16.—Wind shifted to N., clouds moving from W. to E.; thunder audible two or three times to the southward; sky becoming densely overcast, with an occasional shower about nine A.M. We finished up the remains of the Rajah for dinner yesterday. King was fortunate enough to shoot a crow this morning. The rain kept all hands in, pounding and cleaning seed during the morning. The weather cleared up towards the middle of the day, and a brisk breeze sprang up in the south, lasting till near sunset, but rather irregular in its force. Distant thunder was audible to westward and southward frequently during the afternoon.

Monday, June 17.—Night very boisterous and stormy. Northerly wind blowing in squalls, and heavy showers of rain with thunder in the north and west. Heavy clouds moving rapidly from north to south; gradually clearing up during the morning, the wind continuing squally during the day from west and north-west. King out in the afternoon for nardoo.

Tuesday, June 18.—Exceedingly cold night. Sky clear,

slight breeze, very chilly and changeable; very heavy dew. After sunrise cir.-st. clouds began to pass over from west to east, gradually becoming more dense, and assuming the form of cum.-st. The sky cleared, and it became warmer towards noon.

Wednesday, June 19.—Night calm; sky during first part overcast with cir.-cum. clouds, most of which cleared away towards morning, leaving the air much colder, but the sky remained more or less hazy all night, and it was not nearly as cold as last night. About eight o'clock a strong southerly wind sprang up, which enabled King to blow the dust out of our nardoo seeds, but made me too weak to render him any assistance.

Thursday, June 20.—Night and morning very cold, sky clear. I am completely reduced by the effects of the cold and starvation. King gone out for nardoo. Mr. Burke at home pounding seed; he finds himself getting very weak in the legs. King holds out by far the best; the food seems to agree with him pretty well. Finding the sun come out pretty warm towards noon, I took a sponging all over, but it seemed to do little good beyond the cleaning effects, for my weakness is so great that I could not do it with proper expedition. I cannot understand this nardoo at all; it certainly will not agree with me in any form. We are now reduced to it alone, and we manage to get from four to five pounds per day between us.

Friday, June 21.—Last night was cold and clear, winding up with a strong wind from N.E. in the morning. I feel much weaker than ever, and can scarcely crawl out of the Mia Mia. Unless relief comes in some form or other, I cannot possibly last more than a fortnight. It is a great consolation, at least, in this position of ours, to know that we have done all we could, and that our deaths will rather be the result of the mismanagement of others than of any rash acts of our own. Had we come to grief elsewhere, we could only have blamed ourselves; but here we are, returned to Cooper's Creek, where we had every reason to look for provisions and clothing; and yet we have to die of starvation, in spite of the explicit instructions given by Mr. Burke, that the depôt party should await our return, and the strong recommendation to the Committee that we should be followed up by a party from Menindie. At about noon a change of wind took place, and it blew almost as hard from the west as it did previously from the north-east. A few cir.-cum. continued to pass over towards east.

Saturday, June 22.—Night cloudy and warm. Every appearance of rain. Thunder once or twice during the night. Clouds moving in an easterly direction. Lower atmosphere perfectly calm. There were a few drops of rain during the night, and in the morning, about nine A.M., there was every prospect of more rain until towards noon, when the sky cleared up for a time. Mr. Burke and King ou for nardoo. The former returned much fatigued. I am so weak to-day as to be unable to get on my feet.

Sunday, June 23.—All hands at home. I am so weak as to be incapable of crawling out of the Mia Mia. King holds out well, but Mr. Burke finds himself weaker every day.

Monday, June 24.—A fearful night. At about an hour before sunset, a southerly gale sprang up and continued throughout the greater portion of the night; the cold was intense, and it seemed as if one would be shrivelled up. Towards morning it fortunately lulled a little, but a strong cold breeze continued till near sunset, after which it became perfectly calm. King went out for nardoo, in spite of the wind, and came in with a good load, but he himself terribly cut up. He says that he can no longer keep up the work, and as he and Mr. Burke are both getting rapidly weaker, we have but a slight chance of anything but starvation, unless we can get hold of some blacks.

Tuesday, June 25.—Night calm, clear, and intensely cold, especially towards morning. Near daybreak, King reported seeing a moon in the east, with a haze of light stretching up from it; he declared it to be quite as large as the moon, and not dim at the edges. I am so weak that any attempt to get a sight of it was out of the question ; but I think it must have been Venus in the zodiacal light that he saw, with a corona around her. Mr. Burke and King remain at home cleaning and pounding seed. They are both getting weaker every day. The cold plays the deuce with us, from the small amount of clothing we have. My wardrobe consists of a wideawake, a merino shirt, a regatta shirt without sleeves, the remains of a pair of flannel trousers, two pairs of socks in rags, and a waist-coat of which I have managed to keep the pockets together. The others are no better off. Besides these, we have between us, for bedding, two small camel pads, some horse-hair, two or three little bits of rag, and pieces of oilcloth saved from the fire. The day turned out nice and warm.

CHAPTER XIII.

Burke and King resolve on making a last Effort to find the Blacks—
Their Reluctance to leave Wills—His last Entries in the Journal
—His Death—Burke's last Journey—His failing Strength—
He becomes utterly exhausted the second Day—His heroic
Efforts—His last Moments—his Death.

MR. WILLS being at last reduced to a state of such
extreme weakness as to be unable to get on his feet,
or to crawl out of the Mia Mia, or gunyah, the hopes
of the poor sufferers were reduced to the lowest ebb.
King still continued gathering and pounding the
nardoo, and Mr. Burke rendered what assistance he
could; but became at last so weak, that he said he
could be of little use in pounding. King was then
obliged to gather and pound for all three of them,
and he continued to do so for some time; at last
his strength also failed, and he was obliged to lie up
for three or four days, compelling the party to consume a small stock of food which they had laid by
in case of emergency. Under these circumstances,
Mr. Burke proposed, as a last chance, that as much
nardoo as possible should be collected and pounded

in three days, and that he and King should make another effort to find the blacks, as the only means in their power of averting death from starvation.

Mr. Wills, as will be seen from the following entries, joined in this view, and during the three or four days which elapsed before putting it in execution, Mr. Burke repeatedly asked him whether he still wished it, as under no other circumstances would they leave him. To this he finally replied that he looked upon their doing so as the only chance that remained for the whole party, and causing the remainder of his field-books to be buried outside the gunyah, he gave Mr. Burke a letter and his watch for his father, requesting that if King survived Mr. Burke, he would attend to his last wishes in delivering them.

Wednesday, June 26, 1861.—Calm night ; sky overcast with hazy cum. strat. clouds. An easterly breeze sprang up towards morning, making the air much colder. After sunrise there were indications of a clearing up of the sky, but it soon clouded in again, the upper current continuing to move in an easterly direction, whilst a breeze from the E. and N.E. blew pretty regularly throughout the day. Mr. Burke and King are preparing to go up the creek in search of the blacks. They will leave me some nardoo, wood, and water, with which I must do the best I can until they return. I think this is almost our only chance. I feel myself, if anything, rather better, but I cannot say stronger. The nardoo is beginning to agree better with me ; but without some change I see little chance for any

10—2

of us. They have both shown great hesitation and reluctance with regard to leaving me, and have repeatedly
desired my candid opinion in the matter. I could only
repeat, however, that I considered it our only chance, for
I could not last long on the nardoo, even if a supply could
be kept up.

Thursday, June 27.—Cloudy, calm, and comparatively
warm night ; clouds almost stationary. In the morning a
gentle breeze from east. Sky partially cleared up during
the day, making it pleasantly warm and bright; it remained clear during the afternoon and evening, offering
every prospect of a clear, cold night.

Friday, June 28.—Clear, cold night; slight breeze from
the E. ; day beautifully warm and pleasant. Mr. Burke
suffers greatly from the cold, and is getting extremely
weak. He and King start to-morrow up the creek to look
for the blacks; it is the only chance we have of being
saved from starvation. I am weaker than ever, although
I have a good appetite and relish the nardoo much ; but it
seems to give us no nutriment, and the birds here are so
shy as not to be got at. Even if we got a good supply of
fish, I doubt whether we could do much work on them and
the nardoo alone. Nothing now but the greatest good luck
can save any of us ; and as for myself, I may live four or
five days if the weather continues warm. My pulse is at
forty-eight, and very weak, and my legs and arms are
nearly skin and bone. I can only look out, like Mr.
Micawber, "for something to turn up." Starvation on
nardoo is by no means very unpleasant, but for the weakness one feels, and the utter inability to move oneself; for
as far as appetite is concerned, it gives me the greatest
satisfaction. Certainly, fat and sugar would be more to
one's taste; in fact, those seem to me to be the great

stand-by for one in this extraordinary continent; not that
I mean to depreciate the farinaceous food, but the want of
sugar and fat in all substances obtainable here is so great
that they become almost valueless to us as articles of food,
without the addition of something else.

(Signed)   W. J. WILLS.

And thus, fitly closing with his own great name,
the diary of the brave man ended.

Few will read this touching narrative without deep
emotion at the struggles and sufferings it records,
and feelings of admiration for the many virtues displayed by the heroic writer, who relinquished his
duties only with his life.   His patience, and devotion
to his leader; his fidelity and cheerfulness in the
discharge of every duty entrusted to him, are so
conspicuous throughout every page of his affecting
journal, that no further observations of mine are
needful.   The growing peace of mind, which seems
in mercy to have been given to sustain his departing
spirit, shines out more and more clearly towards
the end; and the latest strength of the devoted
martyr is exerted in carefully recording such information as he considers may hereafter be useful to
the cause of science, or to those who may venture
on a like perilous journey in the wilderness.   The
care with which he registers each little incident on
this last day, and the almost pleasant tone in which
he alludes to the chance of " something turning up,"
must strike every reader with admiration; while the

accuracy of his prediction as to the length of time he would probably live, may serve once more to remind us that—

> " There are more things in heaven and earth
> Than are dreamt of in our philosophy."

When King returned, four days afterwards, he found poor Wills lying dead in his gunyah, and he buried him lightly in the sand.

We have no record of Mr. Wills' feelings on entering the dark valley of the shadow of death, and no ostentatious display of religious feeling is made in the pages of the explorers' journal; but we know, from another source,[*] that the tribute due from the creature to the Creator was never forgotten by them in their wanderings: they remembered in whose hands they were, and it may be confidently hoped that when the last struggle came, the still small voice whispered, as of old, in the dying man's ear, " Fear thou not, for I am with thee; be not dismayed, for I am thy God: I will strengthen thee; yea, I will help thee; yea, I will uphold thee with the right hand of my righteousness."

In the meantime, Mr. Burke had set out with King to try and find the blacks, but had not travelled far before he felt that his little remaining strength was rapidly fading away. He complained of great pain in his legs and back, but with the

---

* King's evidence before Royal Commission, Question 1714.

indomitable perseverance which always distinguished him, and which had already led to the successful accomplishment of his exploring labours, he managed to make a tolerable day's journey. This was on the 29th June. The following morning he seemed better, and said he thought he was getting stronger; but, alas! it was only the last flickering of the lamp of life. After travelling about two miles, he was obliged to say he could go no further; but King, who had already witnessed the almost superhuman exertions Mr. Burke had made on several occasions, encouraged him to make another effort, and by little and little, managed to get him along several times. It is piteous to read of the unfailing constancy with which poor Mr. Burke answered these calls upon him, although he must have known he was then dying. But every step he took in advance was a chance for Mr. Wills, and he never flinched from his duty while power was left him to raise a limb. "He walked till he dropped."* At last he said he could not carry his swag, and threw all he had away. See how gradually

"Death came softly stealing on;
How silently!"

Again starting, he soon wished to halt for the night; but as the place was close to a large sheet of water, and exposed to the wind, King prevailed upon him to go a little farther to a more sheltered spot,

* Royal Commission, Question 1066.

where they at last made their camp. Having nothing to eat, they searched about, and found a few small patches of nardoo, which King collected and pounded; and shooting a crow besides, they made their last meal together.

And now the hour had come. Mr. Burke, who had gradually been getting worse, at length told King he felt convinced he could not last many hours longer, requesting him to give his watch and pocket-book to Sir William Stawell, and adding, " I hope you will remain with me here until I am quite dead. It is a comfort to know that some one is by; but when I am dying, it is my wish that you should place the pistol * in my right hand, and that you leave me unburied as I lie."

Throughout that night he spoke but little, and all was over at an early hour the following morning. In the solitude of the lonely forest he sank gently to his long rest: but underneath him were the Everlasting arms. His cares, his fears, his anxious doubts were over, and his work accomplished.

In his last moments a blessed calmness fell upon him, and with a firm hand he traced a few parting

* He had received a pistol as a parting gift from the inhabitants of Beechworth, when he quitted that district; and being a man of warm feelings towards those to whom he was attached, probably wished to retain possession of it in his last moments, in remembrance of them. Knowing King's weak state, he doubtless wished to spare him the labour of digging a grave. It has already been seen how a delay for that purpose in poor Gray's case, led to Mr. Burke's own untimely death.

words to his sister.   The struggles of his weary pilgrimage ended, his mind was at peace, and in that dread hour his heart was attuned to harmonize with none but pure and holy thoughts.   He thought of the old home at St. Clerans, of his brother, of the nurse who, though he knew it not, had travelled thousands of miles in her old age to see her darling Robert; of all who had at any time been dear to him.   With these and a thousand other sweet memories floating around him, and with the name of his dear sister breathing in low murmurs from his lips, the brave spirit passed into the presence of its Creator.

CHAPTER XIV.

Brahé's Journey towards the Darling—He meets with and joins Wright's Party—Brahé and Wright visit Cooper's Creek; but failing to observe the Traces of Mr. Burke's Return, rejoin their Companions—Brahé arrives in Melbourne, and reports Progress —The Committee of the Royal Society deliberate as to what should be done to rescue Mr. Burke—Their approval of his Measures.

WHILE the melancholy events recorded in the two preceding chapters were taking place, Brahé, who, as has been said, quitted the depôt at Cooper's Creek just seven hours before the return of the party from Carpentaria, continued to travel south with his men for seven days; at the end of that period, meeting Wright's party at Bulloo, the two effected a junction. As will be seen from the following extracts, they visited the *cache* at Cooper's Creek together, but failed to observe any traces of Mr. Burke's return: they found nothing which would have led to the opening of the *cache* and the consequent succour of the brave men then dying of want in the wilderness.

Brahé says, under date 28th April, 1861:

Went very early in search of the horses up the creek. At about daylight I got in sight of them, at the same time observing smoke rising within 300 yards from me, and near the horses. There was not light enough to see well, and I thought I had dropped upon a camp of natives, and resolved to try to obtain some information respecting the Darling party. After going a few yards farther, I saw, to my great surprise, a European advance towards me. It was Mr. Hodgkinson. He led me to Mr. Wright's camp; and after bringing in our party, with horses and camels, &c., I placed myself and party under the orders of Mr. Wright.

Wright, however, states that Brahé joined him on the 29th; which is probably correct, as Brahé's journal was compiled some time after the occurrence of the events it records—partly from recollection, and partly from a few rough notes he had jotted down to assist his memory.

Wright says in his despatch to the Committee, dated 20th June, 1861 :—

With two of the party of eight dead, and a third dying, further advance, or a longer stay at Bulloo amid unfriendly natives, were alike impracticable; and had our cattle been molested by the natives our fate would have been sealed. Dr. Beckler and Mr. Hodgkinson, with myself, were the only healthy members of the party, and I decided upon an immediate retreat to Torowoto, at which place I hoped to recruit the sick, and obtain fresh stores from the Darling.

On the 28th of April, therefore, I packed up, proposing to start next morning; but during the night a bell was heard, and at daylight a mob of horses, recognized as forming part of Mr. Burke's equipment, were seen feeding near the stockade. Shortly afterwards Mr. Brahé came up, and we were gratified to find that he was in charge of a party consisting of Patten, M'Donough, and Botan, with twelve horses and six camels (very much infected with scab), on their way to the Darling, from the depôt established by Mr. Burke at Cooper's Creek.

Mr. Brahé at once placed himself and party under my orders.

The following is from Mr. Wright's diary:—

Monday, April 29, 1861.—*Bulloo.*—The horses were very troublesome during the night, perpetually trying to steal away; and, though closely hobbled, more than once attempting to swim the broad creek. About three A.M. a bell was heard from the south, and a number of dark objects, like cattle, could be dimly seen through the darkness. When daylight broke, these objects were recognized as forming part of the mob of horses taken by Mr. Burke, and shortly afterwards Mr. Brahé came up, and reported that he had just arrived from Cooper's creek, where Mr. Burke had left him on the 16th of December in charge of a depôt consisting of Patten, M'Donough, Botan, six camels, and twelve horses. Mr. Brahé had received instructions to remain at Cooper's Creek for three or four months, but had extended that period to eighteen weeks, and only left when his rations ran short. Previous to leaving he made a cache of provisions, sufficient to enable Mr. Burke and party, if competent to retrace their steps, to reach the Darling. Mr. Brahé had not followed Mr. Burke's track to Bulloo, but had pursued a direct course, and reached the 52nd camp of Mr. Burke, eight miles south of my depôt, in about eighty miles. His horses had been one hundred hours without water, but travelled with much less difficulty than could have been hoped for. On proceeding to Mr. Brahé's camp I found Patten suffering from scurvy to an alarming extent, M'Donough almost unable to work, and Botan complaining. Mr. Brahé placed himself under my orders, and I united the two camps in the course of the morning. Of the camels brought down by Mr. Brahé I found three—Beer, Rowa, and Mustana, suffering severely from scab. The others were in good condition.

At a quarter past five this afternoon Mr. Becker died.

Tuesday, April 30.—*Bulloo.*—The night passed quietly, no signs of natives being near having occurred. Early this morning Mr. Becker was buried, the stockade pulled down, and the logs used to form, as far as possible, a protection to the dead. Mr. Becker's clothes, bédding, tent, &c., being quite unfit for use, were burned, and his other effects placed in a pack for conveyance to Melbourne.

Wednesday, May 1.—*Bulloo.*—Saddling commenced at six A.M., and half-past ten A.M. we left Bulloo on our return to Menindie. Dr. Beckler, Mr. Hodgkinson, Mr. Brahé, Botan, and myself were the only healthy members of the party; and I did not see the utility of pushing on the depôt to Cooper's Creek for the purpose of remaining there the few weeks our stores would last. Our cavalcade made quite an imposing appearance with its twenty-two horses and fifteen camels, and the spirits of the whole party were animated by the prospect of regaining the settled districts. Several stoppages took place during the day, from the necessity of altering the seat of our invalids or re-adjusting loads; and to show that our departure was not unnoticed by the natives, fires sprang up at every mile of our progress until we reached Koorliatto, at a tolerably early hour in the afternoon. Patten was greatly fatigued by his ride.

Thursday, May 2.—Koorliatto.—Spelled at Koorliatto. Got up a tent for Patten.

Friday, May 3.—Koorliatto.—As I was anxious to ascertain, before finally leaving the country, whether Mr. Burke had visited the old depôt at Cooper's Creek between the present date and that on which he left on his advance northward, or whether the stores cached there had been disturbed by the natives, I started with Mr. Brahé and three horses for Cooper' Creek, and reached the head-waters of that creek on Sunday, the 5th, in about seventy miles, steering about W.N.W. I did not find any water throughout that distance, but crossed several fine large gum creeks, and saw an immense number of native dogs. The remainder of the party stayed at Koorliatto.

Wednesday, May 8.—Koorliatto.—This morning I reached the Cooper's Creek depôt, and found no sign of Mr. Burke having visited the creek, or the natives having disturbed the stores. I therefore retraced my steps to the depôt which remained at Koorliatto.

Before the Royal Commission Brahé gave the following evidence:—

When you returned to Cooper's Creek with Wright, how long did you remain there?—I suppose—I could not exactly tell—not more than a quarter of an hour at the depôt.

Did you make any examination about to see who had been there?—Yes; I tied my horse up, and so I believe did Wright, near the cache, and went into the stockade and round it, and examined all the trees.

Could you not discover any tracks?—I saw camel tracks, but supposed them to be our own.

Did you see any impression of human feet? — No impression.

Why?—From the number of rats, and the place being dusty.

Are you bushman enough to be able to follow a track? —Yes.

Have you ever practised it?—Yes, I have, of horses and camels.

Could you tell the difference between the track of a white man and of a native?—Certainly, unless they were barefooted.

Even barefooted?—I should not be able.

You did not discover any track that would lead you to suppose any one had been there?—None. I should certainly have opened the cache if I had thought any one had been there. I thought the natives had been there on account of those three different fire-places.

Did you see any native tracks?—No, not fresh.

At whose instigation did you return after meeting Wright; yours or his?—Mine.

What was the object of that?—I had got right, and Patten he was in the doctor's hands. I thought he required rest there, and would get all right in a fortnight's time. Mr. Wright not having gone to Cooper's Creek, I thought that we could not be better employed than in going back there as a last chance for Mr. Burke.

Had you a lingering suspicion that he might be there? —Yes, there was still a chance.

When you met Mr. Wright, had you then, between the two parties, an abundance of provisions?—I believe so; but I do not know what quantity of provisions Wright had; I never inquired.

Until the time of going back to the Darling, you might

have concluded that there was an abundance?—I do not think there was any to spare at the Darling.

By joining Wright's party, had you nothing additional that you could have taken back to deposit at the cache?—Yes, we could have taken some.

You say, I think, that you had abundance with you when you returned to Cooper's Creek with Mr. Wright?—Yes, we could have taken provisions from Bulloo.

Did it not strike you to do so?—No.

And that it did *not* strike either of them to do so is the most unaccountable part of their whole conduct.

The following is from Wright's examination :—

Brahé joined you on the 29th of April, and on the 1st of May you turned your back upon the creek; that is, two days afterwards?—Yes, I went about twenty miles back.

On the 1st of May you left Bulloo on your return: at that time you had the number of men I have mentioned, viz. yourself, Hodgkinson, Beckler, Smith, Belooch, Brahé, M'Donough, and Dost Mahommed—two of them ailing, and the rest in tolerable health, with abundance of horses and camels, all in good condition, with abundance of provisions; but having got some distance you thought better of it?—I did not think better of it after going some short distance, because it was my intention as soon as Brahé came in to go to Cooper's Creek, which I stated to him.

After going two days' journey, you did return to Cooper's Creek?—I buried Dr. Becker the day after Brahé came, and I shifted the camp about twenty miles farther down the creek, and then went to Cooper's Creek.

Did you take any spare horses with you?—We took a pack-horse.

You did not take any provisions or clothing with you?— No.

How long were you reaching Cooper's Creek?—We reached there on the third day.

What day did you leave?—I do not recollect the day, but the diary will show.

You reached Cooper's Creek on Wednesday, the 8th of May, and you say you found no signs of Mr. Burke having visited the creek, or of natives having disturbed the stores; how did you arrive at that conclusion?—There was no mark above ground showing that any white man had been there. There were two or three fires about the place, which I supposed had been made by blacks: I looked at those fires particularly, and there was not a stick of wood as large as one of the pen-sticks on the table which was not burned; just as a black fellow makes a fire: he just brings what is enough to keep a fire, and no more. I took Brahé there, and told him to take particular notice to see if the place was in the same way he left it; and he looked at it and said it was. The place had been covered over, and everything was so much like he had left it, that he did not know it had been disturbed.

Did you leave any record at Cooper's Creek of your having been there?—No, I did not; I intended doing so, but I thought if I disturbed the place where the things were buried and took the bottle up, the chances were the blacks, as I supposed they had been at the depôt, would discover them. I was not very sure whether they were watching us; we had seen a smoke the night before, and being over cautious, I would not take the bottle up to put a note in it.

There was a mark of the 21st April on the tree, that was left unaltered?—Everything was left just as Brahé left it, according to his account.

If Mr. Burke had returned there, how was he to know anybody had been there?—They could have seen my horse tracks where the things were buried. I remarked to Brahé he ought to have buried those things two or three days before he left, and put the horses in under the shade, as he had been doing before; and I said, "At all events we will put our horses in here now, and let them walk about on it, and the blacks will never think of digging there, if they should happen to be looking about."

Would there have been any difficulty in putting W. for Wright, and the 8th of May under the 21st April?—I could have done that with a knife, if I had had the presence of mind to do so.

You did not go to the creek at all?—No.

You did not make any search, in fact?—I just stayed there, and had a look round about the place; in fact, I first thought of camping there that night; but the horses I had taken with me being horses that had been at Cooper's Creek with Mr. Brahé, he said, "If we stop here to-night the horses will certainly go back five miles up the creek, to the place where they used to run, and we shall have to walk up there in the morning for them:" and I thought it just as well to camp where the horses were used to stop as to camp there. When I saw no marks showing that any white men had been there, I was very anxious to get back to my depôt as soon as I possibly could do so, knowing the state the men were in.

Would it not have been possible to have sent Mr. Brahé, or some other trustworthy person, back to the sick people, and yourself have gone on up to Cooper's Creek, and remained there for some time?—It would have been impossible to have done so.

It will be remembered that twenty-two days after this visit, on the 30th of May, Mr. Wills visited the place for the last time.

Wright and Brahé, having rejoined their companions, proceeded towards Menindie, *via* Torowoto, and reached the Darling on Tuesday, the 18th of June, 1861. Brahé left for Melbourne on Friday, the 21st of June, taking with him an account of his and Wright's proceedings, and such papers as had been addressed to the Committee by Mr. Burke when he quitted Cooper's Creek for Carpentaria on the 16th of December, 1860.

On the morning of the 30th of June, 1861, the day before Mr. Burke's death, Brahé arrived in Melbourne, and delivered his despatches into the hands of Dr. M'Adam, Honorary Secretary to the Committee, who, having been apprised of Brahé's approach by telegram on the previous day, had communicated with Sir Henry Barkly, and arranged to lay the papers before his Excellency and Sir William Stawell at the earliest possible moment. This was accordingly done. The same afternoon (being Sunday) a special meeting of the Committee was held to hear the documents read, and determine what steps should be taken for the relief of the explorers. At this meeting Brahé was examined, and gave an account of all that had occurred within his knowledge up to

11—2

that time.   He explained his reasons for leaving Cooper's Creek before Mr. Burke's return, and gave such additional information, with respect to the habits of the natives and state of the country, as he considered might be useful to any relief-party proceeding in search of his leader.

It will be appropriate in this place to show what were the opinions held at this time by the leading members of the Committee, with regard to those proceedings of Mr. Burke which were found fault with, *after a full knowledge of actual results had been obtained*—results, be it observed, not attributable to any want of care or forethought on the part of Mr. Burke, but arising from the disregard of instructions, and a fatal want of stedfastness, on the part of those to whom he had intrusted the means of affording him relief.

Sir William Stawell (Chief Justice) said :—

A great many difficulties might have met Mr. Burke, any one of which would account for not hearing from him. His men might have been attacked with scurvy, and be still alive, without being able to move any distance ; and they might be in some place waiting the arrival of the rainy season.   That was but one of the thousand chances that might detain him.   Although he (Sir William) was anxious to get the worst from Mr. Brahé, he was not afraid of Mr. Burke after the *wise and careful way he had proceeded to Cooper's Creek*, and *the manner in which he had followed the instructions of the Committee.*   He thought that

Mr. Burke would have satisfied himself that the course north from Cooper's Creek was not practicable; and that then he went to the west, after getting over the Stony Desert. Stuart's country had plenty of water and feed; and it could not be a bad season at which he started; for a fortnight after, Stuart, who had been over the country before, went out a second time. Although they must necessarily feel anxious about Burke and his party, there was no ground for despairing at all. The question was, what steps should they take in order that assistance might reach him as speedily as possible?

Mr. Ligar (Surveyor-General) said—

Looking to what Mr. Burke was about, *he conceived that, on the whole, he had attempted to carry out the instructions of the Committee in the best manner possible.* The first instruction was to make a route to the Gulf of Carpentaria, keeping Stuart's track on his left, and Gregory's on his right: he did it, and failed; and then he tried to get into Stuart's track. He (Mr. Ligar) was convinced that Mr. Burke was in Stuart's country, or he was pushing to where Dr. Mueller and Mr. Gregory went, lower down. What Mr. Brahé had done since parting with Mr. Burke, was a matter the Committee could leave for consideration two or three days hence. It was very interesting, and would make a continuous narrative of the Expedition up to the last that was seen of the leader. What they should rather bend their minds to now was, how to reach Mr. Burke, and succour him. It struck him that Mr. Burke weakened his party by dividing it into three. Thus far he disagreed with him.

Sir William Stawell.—It must not be forgotten that Mr.

Wright and party were to follow the main party with provisions, and join Mr. Burke.

Dr. Mueller urged the necessity of acting promptly; but the party must be sufficiently strong, so that if scurvy attacked them, aid could be detached to attend the sick; which could not be done with a small party—indeed, a small party would be stopped, as Mr. Wright's had been, by sickness. It was necessary to procure the aid of the natives, if possible, for their quick eye would discover traces in the wilderness that no Caucasian eye could discover. It was incumbent on the committee to send aid speedily. Calculating the provisions that Mr. Burke's party had with them, he found that, with the prudence and economy that they might suppose Mr. Burke would practise, they would have average rations for five months. Economizing still more, and with the assistance of game and wild animals the party might procure, the provisions might be made to go still further. Although there was room for great fear and anxiety to be entertained, he did not consider Mr. Burke's case hopeless. Prompt measures should be adopted, as Mr. Burke might find it possible to spin out his rations till succour reached him. Mr. Burke, if tied up, would reasonably expect the Committee would send succour.

Dr. Wilkie pointed out, that when the Expedition first started, there were eighteen men in it. The fact was, that at this moment the Committee had only four men in the field. He thought that, under those circumstances, with the aid of a large vote from the Legislature, that the Committee should provide succour on a liberal scale. They should send a party sufficiently strong to leave a subsidiary party at the depôt, Cooper's Creek, to which they should take stores; so that if Mr. Burke returned, he might be secure. It was incumbent on the Committee to arrange at once to send a large party under Mr. Howitt—say ten or eleven. Mr. Wright's party intended to reach Cooper's Creek in three weeks; when half-way they were attacked by scurvy, and there they remained within 200 miles of Menindie. Mr. Wright could send no one away for succour; and had it not been for the return of the party from Cooper's Creek the whole must have perished. The committee had simply to strengthen Mr. Howitt's party, or to reorganize it with different instructions from those already issued. He could leave four men at Cooper's Creek while he proceeded in search of Mr. Burke with the main strength of his party.

Sir William Stawell thought they should pass the resolution, and settle the strength of the party. That would be something gained, and would enable Mr. Howitt to make despatch with his arrangements next day. Doing something to save a day would be doing a great deal.

Dr. Gillbee thought the proper organization of the party was of more importance than gaining a day; and he moved the adjournment of the meeting till next day, when they would have Mr. Brahé's written statement to guide them; while, in the meantime, Mr. Howitt, as well as the Committee, could give their most earnest consideration to the whole subject.

Sir William Stawell thought it would be a great pity that they should adjourn, having so unusually met on a Sunday, without doing something. (Hear, hear.) All they knew now was that four men whom they sent out required aid. They could arrive at a resolution to send aid, which would enable Mr. Howitt to proceed with his arrangements; they need not settle the number now; they

could determine eventually the minor details.   The men's
lives were depending on a thread, perhaps.*

The above extracts, therefore, go to show that the
very measures subsequently animadverted upon un-
favourably were, on the whole, stamped with the
approval of the Committee as a body at this time.
The report of the Royal Commission will be given at
length in a subsequent chapter, and the reader can
then judge for himself as to the justice or otherwise
of its strictures on the conduct of the brave man who
added millions of habitable acres to the dominion
of his country at the cost of his life.

* In everything connected with this expedition, Sir William
Stawell appears to have been conspicuous throughout for the practical nature of his views, and the energy with which he at all times
urged the necessity of prompt *action*. He it was, who, when the
account of Stuart's discoveries was forwarded to Mr. Burke, wrote at
the same time a private note begging that nothing short of the actual
fulfilment of his mission should cause Mr. Burke to relax in his
efforts to succeed.

CHAPTER XV.

THE Committee, having fully considered the circumstances adverted to in the preceding chapter, determined to lose no time in taking measures for the relief
of Mr. Burke; they accordingly organized a party *
under the leadership of Mr. Howitt, a gentleman
of much experience in the colony, from whose efforts
it was hoped that beneficial results might accrue,
and tidings be obtained of the gallant men in whose
fate the entire colony had now become deeply interested.

Before detailing Mr. Howitt's proceedings, however, it will be necessary to return to King, who,
having done all in his power towards attending to
the last wishes of his chief, whose eyes he had closed

* In addition to this party another was sent round in a steamer to
the Northern Coast, and several search parties were despatched by
the neighbouring Colonies.

in death, had returned to Mr. Wills' gunyah; and, finding him also dead, had buried him as well as he could. He then remained on the spot some days, to recover his own strength. His narrative proceeds:—

Finding that my stock of nardoo was running short, and being unable to gather it, I tracked the natives who had been to the camp by their footprints in the sand, and went some distance down the creek, shooting crows and hawks on the road. The natives, hearing the report of the gun, came to meet me, and took me with them to their camp, giving me nardoo and fish. They took the birds I had shot and cooked them for me, and afterwards showed me a gunyah, where I was to sleep with three of the single men. The following morning they commenced talking to me, and putting one finger on the ground, and covering it with sand, at the same time pointing up the creek, saying, "White fellow," which I understood to mean that one white man was dead. From this I knew that they were the tribe who had taken Mr. Wills' clothes. They then asked me where the third white man was, and I also made the sign of putting two fingers on the ground and covering them with sand, at the same time pointing up the creek. They appeared to feel great compassion for me when they understood that I was alone on the creek, and gave me plenty to eat. After being four days with them, I saw that they were becoming tired of me; and they made signs that they were going up the creek, and that I had better go downwards; but I pretended not to understand them. The same day they shifted camp, and I followed them; and, on reaching their camp, I shot some crows, which pleased them so much that they made me a breakwind in the centre of their camp, and came and sat round me until such time as the crows were cooked, when they assisted me to eat them. The same day, one of the women, to whom I had given part of a crow, came and gave me a ball of nardoo, saying that she would give me more only she had such a sore arm that she was unable to pound. She showed me a sore on her arm, and the thought struck me that I would boil some water in the billy and wash her arm with a sponge. During the operation the whole tribe sat round, and were muttering one to another. Her husband sat down by her side, and she was crying all the time. After I had washed it, I touched it with some nitrate of silver, when she began to yell, and ran off, crying out, "Mokow! mokow!" (Fire! fire!) From this time, she and her husband used to give me a small quantity of nardoo both night and morning, and whenever the tribe were about going on a fishing excursion, he used to give me notice to go with them. They also used to assist me in making a gourley, or breakwind, whenever they shifted camp. I generally shot a crow or a hawk, and gave it to them in return for these little services. Every four or five days the tribe would surround me, and ask whether I intended going up or down the creek; at last I made them understand that if they went up I should go up the creek, and if they went down I should also go down; and from this time they seemed to look upon me as one of themselves, and supplied me with fish and nardoo regularly.

They were very anxious, however, to know where Mr. Burke lay; and one day when we were fishing in the water-holes close by I took them to the spot. On seeing his remains the whole party wept bitterly, and covered them with bushes. After this they were much kinder to me than before; and I always told them that the white men would be here before two moons; and in the even-

ings, when they came with nardoo and fish, they used
to talk about the "white fellows" coming, at the same
time pointing to the moon. I also told them they would
receive many presents, and they constantly asked me for
tomahawks, called by them "bomayko." From this time
to when the relief party arrived—a period of about a
month—they treated me with uniform kindness, and
looked upon me as one of themselves. The day on which
I was released, one of the tribe who had been fishing came
and told me that the white fellows were coming, and the
whole of the tribe who were then in camp sallied out in
every direction to meet the party, while the man who had
brought me the news took me across the creek, where I
shortly saw the party coming down.

Mr. Howitt, then, as has been said, being despatched
with a relieving party, proceeded on his mission; and
from his interesting diary the following passages are
taken, as affording, in conjunction with the papers
which follow, the fittest conclusion to the story which
these pages are intended to record.

September 3, Camp 21.—Lat. 28° 22'. *Long.* 142° 31'.
—Started at eight o'clock, and left the Expedition track at
Poria Creek. Struck a course for Cooper's Creek N.W. by
compass. For seven miles travelled over sand-ridges running N.E. and S.W., with wide clayey valleys between, in
which were occasional small pools of muddy water. The
feed everywhere very dry, but tolerably plentiful on the
sand-hills. Bushes and small mulgar-trees were growing
in places. We here crossed a dry box swamp, where
crows, wood swallows, kites, and small birds were numerous; and I observed here several trees with a rough bark

resembling cork, and with bunches of long pointed dark green leaves growing at the ends of the small branches. The sand-hills here became low and flat, and the valley wider. Shortly afterwards crossed the track of a large camel going N.E., apparently about eight months ago. The country undulating and well grassed, and, as far as I could make out, the watershed both to the N.E. and S.W. At twelve o'clock, after crossing a dry swamp full of water-courses, and passing a low sand-hill, came on a creek running S.W., thickly timbered with large box-trees, the bed wide and the banks steep, and in several places large pools of clear water. Marshmallows and other vegetation, now perfectly dried up, were on the banks. Native camps were numerous; but none that I saw were very recent. Mussel-shells and the claws of crayfish were lying near them. I have every reason to believe that some of these pools are permanent. Crossing this we passed several branch creeks running through a clayey plain, and all lined with trees; large pools of water in several. I named this creek after the Hon. David Wilkie, M.D., M.L.C. On leaving the clay flats at the creek we again crossed sand-hills and un-dulating country for several miles, mostly well grassed, but much burned up. Salt-bush and cotton-bush plentiful in the hollows, and scattered timber beginning to appear. At half-past two came on a water-course running N., and containing large but shallow pools of water. The feed round about excellent, and enough timber to be called a thin gum forest. The gums here a new species not before seen by us, several feet of the butt having a rough semi-persistent bark, above which it is smooth and greenish, with a red tint; leaves thick and glossy, very much resembling one growing near Omeo. Ducks here very tame. Camped, having made eighteen miles, and

country not looking so well ahead. The general fall seems
to be to the westward. Samla, the largest of our camels,
lay down just before reaching the camp ; he is the only
one of the lot that has not improved in condition, and he
keeps himself poor by constantly watching the other camels,
and driving them away from the females. He only carries
two cwts.

September 6, Camp 24—Lat. 28°. *Long.* 142° 2'.—
Left camp shortly after six. The horses had not fed during the night, partly from thirst, partly being afraid of
the stones. Followed down a gully leading into very
stony plains, which we crossed for several hours, being
obliged to lead the horses very slowly. No timber, and
scarcely any vegetation ; the most desolate stony wilderness imaginable. About ten o'clock came near the sand-
hills, and the country improved as regarded travelling, but
not for feed or water. On a dry watercourse came on a
party of natives, of whom some ran away ; the others,
consisting of an old grey-haired man, an old hag of a
woman, a younger man, and two or three lubras and children, waited until I rode up. They were in a very excited
state, waving branches, and jabbering incessantly. The
younger man shook all over with fright. Sandy could
not understand them, and I could only catch " Gow " (Go
on). At last, by the offer of a knife, I prevailed on the
old man to come with us to show us the nearest water,
but after half a mile his courage gave way, and he climbed
up a box-tree to be out of reach. Mr. Brahé rode up to
him, when he climbed into the top branches, jabbering
without stopping for a moment. Finding that he would not
come down, and kept pointing to the N.W. (our course), we
left him. All the natives were naked, and the old man was
the only one who had any covering for his head—a net.

We here entered undulating sandy country, slightly
scrubbed and well grassed, and at the same time came
on Brahé's down track. Our horses at once struck into
a better pace, going at least three miles and a-half an
hour. The camels also pushed on well. The loose horses
kept wide of the track, looking out for water in the polygonum ground, and at ten minutes past twelve one old
stager found an ample supply in a channel on the right
hand. The horses at once made a rush, and it was almost
impossible to prevent them drinking as much as they
wished. Three had for the last hour shown unmistakable
signs of giving in, and all were very much pinched with
thirst. Camped by the water, in first-rate feed. Rain
came on steadily from N.E. shortly after, and has continued. The horses have just been a third time to water.

September 9, *Camp* 26.—*Lat.* 27° 49′. *Long.* 141° 38′.
—While loading up this morning, five black fellows made
their appearance on the opposite side of the creek, and, as
usual, commenced shouting and waving their arms. We
cooeyd in return, and one waded across, but waited on the
bank until I broke a branch and beckoned him to come
up. The others then followed him. They were all fine,
well-built young men, with open, intelligent faces, and
very different from the natives usually met with. They
wore nets wrapped round their waists ; and one, apparently the head man, had his front teeth knocked out.
Sandy said he could only understand "narrangy word"
they said ; but I believe that he could not understand
them at all, as he was quite unable to make them com-
prehend that I wished to know if they had seen any stray
camels about the creek. Before we had finished loading
they returned to the opposite bank, and sat down watching us. On our starting, they waded across to our camp

—probably to pick up anything left behind, which would be very little. To-day we travelled over earthy plains for thirteen miles ; they were cracked in every direction, and covered with a network of channels. In times of flood the whole of them must be under water, and I can scarcely imagine anything more luxuriant than the appearance of these plains after a wet season. At present everything is dry and withered, but everywhere the stalks of marsh-mallows and other flowering plants are as high as a horse's back, and very close together. Tufts of grass line each side, and cover the bed of the water-courses. Here and there clumps and lines of timber mark the course of the larger creeks, and sand-hills rise like islands from the plains. To the S. of W., at about nine miles, we had a range—probably stony—and following its base a strongly-marked line of timber, which I believe to be the main creek. No floods appear to have come down for two seasons, and water-holes which were tolerably well filled five months ago are now dry, or nearly so. At thirteen miles crossed a branch, where Burke's marked tree, LXI, stands, and camped at a clay pan under a sand-hill, about a mile to the W. Strong breeze from the N.E. and N. all day, and steady rain at night. Near here, I observed for the first time a new tree, with a rough scaly bark and thick foliage, the leaves small and oval, and set in pairs on a stem. The tree grows to fifteen or twenty feet, and bears numbers of flat brown pods, each containing from five to six hard light brown beans, known by us as the bean-tree.

September 10, *Camp* 27.—*Lat.* 27° 39′. *Long.* 141° 30′. —The rain ceased shortly before sunrise, and the travelling was, in consequence, very heavy, the earthy plains being not only soft, as before, but sticky. Shortly after leaving

camp saw several natives on a sand-hill making signs.
I went up to them with Mr. Welch, and after a great
deal of trouble persuaded one to come to me. He was
a fine-looking fellow, painted white, skeleton fashion, and
carried a very long boomerang stuck in his girdle behind.
I could make nothing of him, excepting that he gave me
a small ball of what seemed to be chewed grass, as a
token of friendship, and in return I gave him a piece of
cold doughboy I had with me for lunch, which he seemed
to relish very much. We travelled till noon over a suc-
cession of earthy plains, broken by numerous box channels,
one of which contained a large reach of water; but the
feed everywhere was miserably dry and scarce. The
country looks wretched. After passing this channel, seven
natives made their appearance, one of whom Mr. Brahé
recognized as one of the party who tried to surprise the
depôt last season. They presented him with a small
quantity of some dried plant, from a bundle which one
of them carried; it had a strong pungent taste and smell,
and I am at a loss to conjecture its use, unless as a kind
of tobacco. Our black boy was frightened, and told me
he thought they meant to "look out, kill him"—as I
understood—by witchcraft, or enchantment, or poison.
They followed us at a distance to our camp, where they
sat down a little way off, making signs that they were
hungry, and wanted tomahawks. After an hour's waiting
they decamped. Killed two deaf adders and a snake of a
sulphur colour on the track. Halted near a small pool
of water, where there was a little green feed, which has
become a rarity; the country looks miserable ahead.
Travelling very heavy on the horses, as the mud balls
in great lumps. Stony ridges to the S. of the creek, at
about four miles, and a good deal of timber visible on

12

all sides. Weather still threatening rain ; flies very
troublesome.

September 13, *Camp* 30.—*Lat.* 27° 38'. *Long.* 141°.—
Made a short stage to-day, for the sake of feed for the
horses, which is a thing to be considered, from the dry
appearance of the country. Reached the depôt, Fort
Wills, in three miles, through country rather better than
we have seen for some days. More rain has fallen here
lately than elsewhere, and the grass is just springing, but
too short to be of much use. I believe this to be the first
rain for many months. The water all down the creek, as
far as we have come, has fallen at the rate of about three
feet in the last four months. Found the depôt as Mr.
Brahé left it, the plant untouched, and nothing removed
of the useless things lying about, but a piece of leather.
But from the very evident fact that these things are
buried, I cannot understand why the natives have not
found them. From here followed down the creek for
several miles, and camped at some sand-hills near a pool
of water. Saw here the track of a large camel going up
the creek. The small crested pigeon, spoken of by Sturt,
numerous. Cool wind from S.E.

September 14, *Camp* 31.—*Lat.* 27° 42'. *Long.* 140° 4'.
—Camped on a large water-hole, about a quarter of a mile
below Mr. Burke's first camp after leaving the depôt. We
could see where the camels had been tied up, but found
no marked tree. To-day I noticed in two or three places
old camel droppings and tracks, where Mr. Brahé informed
me he was certain their camels had never been, as they
were watched every day near the depôt, and tied up at
night. Mr. Burke's camels were led on the way down.
It looked very much as if stray camels had been about
during the last four months. The tracks seemed to me to

be going up the creek, but the ground was too stony to be able to make sure.

September 15, *Camp* 32.—*Lat.* 27° 44′. *Long.* 140° 40′. —On leaving this morning I went ahead with Sandy, to try and pick up Mr. Burke's track. At the lower end of a large water-hole, found where one or two horses had been feeding for some months; the tracks ran in all directions to and from the water, and were as recent as a week. At the same place I found the handle of a clasp-knife. From here struck out south for a short distance from the creek, and found a distinct camel's track and droppings on a native path : the footprint was about four months old, and going E. I then set the black boy to follow the creek, and struck across some sandy country in a bend on the north side. No tracks here ; and coming on a native path leading my way, I followed it, as the most likely place to see any signs. In about four miles this led me to the lower end of a very large reach of water, and on the opposite side were numbers of native wurleys. I crossed at a neck of sand, and at a little distance again came on the track of a camel going up the creek ; at the same time I found a native, who began to gesticulate in a very excited manner, and to point down the creek, bawling out, " Gow, gow ! " as loud as he could ; when I went towards him he ran away, and finding it impossible to get him to come to me, I turned back to follow the camel track and to look after my party, as I had not seen anything of them for some miles. The track was visible in sandy places, and was evidently the same I had seen for the last two days. I also found horse tracks in places, but very old. Crossing the creek, I cut our track, and rode after the party. In doing so I came upon three pounds of tobacco, which had lain where I saw it for some

12—2

time. This, together with the knife-handle, the fresh horse tracks, and the camel track going eastward, puzzled me extremely, and led me into a hundred conjectures. At the lower end of the large reach of water before mentioned I met Sandy and Frank looking for me, with the intelligence that King, the only survivor of Mr. Burke's party, had been found. A little farther on I found the party halted, and immediately went across to the blacks' wurleys, where I found King sitting in a hut which the natives had made for him. He presented a melancholy appearance—wasted to a shadow, and hardly to be distinguished as a civilized being but by the remnants of clothes upon him. He seemed exceedingly weak, and found it occasionally difficult to follow what he said. The natives were all gathered round, seated on the ground, looking with a most gratified and delighted expression. Camped where the party had halted on a high bank, close to the water. I shall probably be here ten days, to recruit King before returning.

September 16, *Camp* 32.—King already looks vastly improved, even since yesterday, and not like the same man. Have commenced shoeing horses and preparing for our return. Wind from S.W., with signs of rain. The natives seem to be getting ready for it.

September 18, *Camp* 32.—Left camp this morning with Messrs. Brahé, Welch, Wheeler, and King, to perform a melancholy duty which has weighed on my mind ever since we have camped here, and which I have only put off until King should be well enough to accompany us. We proceeded down the creek for seven miles, crossing a branch running to the southward, and followed a native track leading to that part of the creek where Mr. Burke, Mr. Wills, and King camped after their unsuccessful

attempt to reach Mount Hopeless, and the northern settlements of South Australia, and where poor Wills died.
We found the two gunyahs pretty much as King had
described them, situated on a sand-bank between two
water-holes, and about a mile from the flat where they
procured the nardoo seed, on which they managed to exist
so long. Poor Wills' remains we found lying in the wurley
in which he died, and where King, after his return from
seeking for the natives, had buried him with sand and
rushes. We carefully collected the remains and interred
them where they lay; and, not having a prayer-book, I
read chap. xv. of 1 Cor., that we might at least feel a
melancholy satisfaction in having shown the last respect
to his remains. We heaped sand over the grave, and laid
branches upon it, that the natives might understand by
their own tokens not to disturb the last repose of a fellow-
being. I cut the following inscription on a tree close by,
to mark the spot:—

> W. J. WILLS,
> XLV. Yds.
> W.N.W.
> A.H.

The field-books, a note-book belonging to Mr. Burke,
various small articles lying about, of no deep value in
themselves, but now invested with an interest from the circumstances connected with them, and some of the nardoo
seed on which they had subsisted, with the small wooden
trough in which it had been cleansed, I have now in my
possession. We returned home with saddened feelings;
but I must confess that I felt a sense of relief that this
painful ordeal had been gone through. King was very

tired when we returned, and I must most unwillingly
defer my visit to the spot where Mr. Burke's remains are
lying until he is better able to bear the fatigue.

September 19.—Shoeing horses. A very slow and troublesome job, as many have never been shod before, and
our forge is of the most primitive description. This afternoon got the pigeons in order of flying. Their tails being
rubbed down by travelling so far in a cage, I got the tails
from several crested pigeons, and inserted feathers in the
stumps of our carriers, fastening the splices with waxed
thread. The plan answered far better than I had expected,
and the birds can now fly about the aviary we have made
of a tent with the greatest ease.

September 20.—Started the pigeons at daybreak, each
with a message fastened to its legs. On throwing them
up they commenced wheeling round the camp, but separated, one being chased by one of the large kites which
are always hovering about the creek. After flying round
in various directions with great speed they gradually drew
across the creek, when we lost sight of three; the fourth,
after making a large circle, pitched in a tree about a mile
off. After breakfast he was found under a bush, with a
kite watching him; and the feathers of one of the other
pigeons was found not far off, having been killed. Of the
two others nothing has been seen, and I hope that they
got clear away, but I am much afraid that the experiment
has proved a failure; however, I should have thought
more of it if the pigeons had made a more decided start.
Last night the wind changed from N.E. to S.W., and
brought up a slight shower. This morning S.W., with
heavy clouds, threatening rain. King improving slowly
but very weak. Turned out the white pigeon again this
afternoon; he flew into a gum standing in the camp, and

has taken up his quarters there—not a proper proceeding for a carrier pigeon, according to my ideas.

September 21.—Finding it would not be prudent for King to go out for two or three days, I could no longer defer making a search for the spot where Mr. Burke died; and with such directions as King could give, I went up the creek this morning with Messrs. Brahé, Welsh, Wheeler, and Aitkin. We searched the creek upwards for eight miles, and, at length, strange to say, found the remains of Mr. Burke lying among tall plants under a clump of box-trees, within 200 yards of our last camp, and not thirty paces from our track. It was still more extraordinary that three or four of the party and the two black boys had been close to the spot without noticing it. The bones were entire, with the exception of the hands and feet; and the body had been removed from the spot where it first lay, and where the natives had placed branches over it, to about five paces distance. I found the revolver which Mr. Burke held in his hand when he expired, partly covered with leaves and earth, and corroded with rust. It was loaded and capped. We dug a grave close to the spot, and interred the remains wrapped in the union jack—the most fitting covering in which the bones of a brave but unfortunate man could take their last rest. On a box-tree, at the head of the grave, the following inscription is cut:—

> R. O'H. B.
> 21 | 9 '61.
> A. H.

September 22.—The pigeon still keeps its quarters at the camp, and comes down to feed now and then. I have removed the message, and shall leave it to its fate. It has been trying hard to rain for two or three days, but does not seem able ; great clouds drift over, looking ready to burst, but only squeeze out two or three drops, and then pass over. I expect fully that it will clear up without rain ; another dry season will make Cooper's Creek look fearfully miserable. When the hot weather comes on the water-holes, many of them will be dry, unless filled by rain or a flood. I have written down King's narrative as much as possible in his own words. Shall annex it to this diary. Finished shoeing the horses.

September 23.—Went down the creek to-day, in search of the natives. One of the party accompanied me, and we took two days' rations, in case it should be necessary to prolong our search. Two days after we camped here the natives left, and have not been seen since ; and I could not think of leaving without showing them that we could appreciate and reward the kindness they had shown to Burke's party, and particularly to King. For three miles we travelled over alluvial flats along the creek, timbered with box and large gums, and dotted with bean-trees, orange-trees of large size, but at present without fruit, various kinds of acacias, and other bushes. To the right hand, level flats and sand-ridges, apparently tolerably grassed. We then came on a large reach of water, where four or five natives had just been fishing ; their nets were lying on the sand to dry, and the fire yet burning. Not seeing any one about, and getting no answer to a cooey, we went on. At three miles more we passed the first feeder of Stralezki's Creek, going to the southward ; and at a large reach of water below, found the natives camped. They made a great commotion when we rode up, but seemed very friendly. I unpacked my blanket, and took out specimens of the things I intended giving them—a tomahawk, a knife, beads, a looking-glass, comb, and flour and sugar. The tomahawk was the great object of attraction, after that the knife, but I think that the looking-glass surprised them most. On seeing their faces, some seemed dazzled, others opened their eyes like saucers, and made a rattling noise with their tongues expressive of surprise. We had quite a friendly palaver, and my watch amused them immensely. When I gave them some of the sugar to taste, it was absurd to see the sleight of hand with which they pretended to eat it, I suppose from a fear of being poisoned, which I suppose is general, as our black boys are continually in dread lest the " wild black fellow " should poison them by some means. I made them understand that they were to bring the whole tribe up next morning to our camp to receive their presents, and we parted the best of friends. The names of the principal men are Tchukulow, Mungallee (three in number), Toquunter, Pitchery (three in number, one a funny little man, with his head in a net and a kite's feather in it; another, a tall man, with his beard tied in a point), Pruriekow, and Borokow.

September 24.—This morning, about ten o'clock, our black friends appeared in a long procession, men, women, and children, or, as they here also call them, piccaninnies; and at a mile distance they commenced bawling at the top of their voices as usual. When collected altogether on a little flat, just below our camp, they must have numbered between thirty and forty, and the uproar was deafening. With the aid of King, 1 at last got them all seated before me, and distributed the presents —tomahawks, knives, necklaces, looking-glasses, combs— among them. I think no people were ever so happy before, and it was very interesting to see how they pointed out one or another who they thought might be overlooked. The piccaninnies were brought forward by their parents to have red ribbon tied round their dirty little heads. One old woman, Carrawaw, who had been particularly kind to King, was loaded with things. I then divided 50 lbs. of sugar between them, each one taking his share in a union-jack pocket handkerchief, which they were very proud of. The sugar soon found its way into their mouths ; the flour, 50 lbs. of which I gave them, they at once called " white-fellow nardoo," and they explained that they understood that these things were given to them for having fed King. Some old clothes were then put on some of the men and women, and the affair ended in several of our party and several of the black-fellows having an impromptu " corroboree," to the intense delight of the natives, and, I must say, very much to our own amuse-ment. They left, making signs expressive of friendship, carrying their presents with them. The men all wore a net girdle; and of the women, some wore one of leaves, others of feathers. I feel confident that we have left the best impression behind us, and that the " white-fellows," as they have already learned to call us, will be looked on henceforth as friends, and that, in case of emergency, any one will receive the kindest treatment at their hands.

September 25, *at Camp* 31.—This morning I turned my face homewards. The object of our mission being fulfilled, I had to do so, but I return with a great regret at not being able to go on. We take back five months' rations from this date, at the scale we have been using, and which has proved sufficient. The party are in the best of health, the horses in fine order, and the camels none the worse for their journey, and decidedly in better health than when they left the Darling. On the edge of a country so well worth exploring, in a tolerably good season, and with the means I now have at my disposal, I feel how much might be done. We camped to-day at our last camp but one coming down the creek, making an easy stage for King. Got in by noon, as the horses were very fresh after their spell. The camels gave us a good deal of trouble this afternoon, and from a cause which may and probably will constantly occur. One of the male camels had taken to driving the females about, and fighting with the other male, Sama, who up to this time had been master. To-day, the other camel was furious; and in spite of being short-hobbled, and having his head tied down to his knee, chased the whole of the camels from the camp, ten minutes after they were let loose; and although Brahé went immediately after them, and was for three hours on their tracks, he was unable to overtake them. Coming back for a horse, he took Sandy with him, and cut across to where he had left the tracks, running north over some very rough stony country. It was dark before they returned, having found the camels some miles away. From this and similar occurrences, I find it very unwise to take male and female camels together on a journey. One is never safe for a day from their straying, and from continual fights between the male camels for mastery. The result is, that the camels are continually harassed, and watch each other instead of feeding. With either all male or all female camels, there would be less, or certainly not more, trouble than with horses; and with this drawback, I firmly believe in the suitability of camels for exploring.

CHAPTER XVI.

Report of the Royal Commission—Despatch from the Government of
Victoria—Reply of the Duke of Newcastle.

VICTORIA: By the Grace of God, of the United King-
dom of Great Britain and Ireland, Queen, Defender
of the Faith.

To our trusty and well-beloved the Honourable Sir
THOMAS SIMSON PRATT, K.C.B., the Honourable
Sir FRANCIS MURPHY, Speaker of our Legislative
Assembly, the Honourable MATTHEW HERVEY, M.P.,
the Honourable JAMES FORESTER SULLIVAN, M.P.,
and EVELYN PITFIELD SHIRLEY STURT, Esquire, all
of Melbourne, in the colony of Victoria, GREETING:

WHEREAS the Governor of our Colony of Victoria, with the
advice of the Executive Council thereof, has deemed it
expedient that a Commission should forthwith issue for the
purpose of inquiring into all the circumstances connected
with the sufferings and death of ROBERT O'HARA BURKE
and WILLIAM JOHN WILLS, the Victorian explorers: AND
WHEREAS it is desirable to ascertain the true causes of this
lamentable result of the Expedition to the said ROBERT

O'HARA BURKE and his companions: AND especially to
investigate the circumstances under which the depôt at
Cooper's Creek was abandoned by WILLIAM BRAHÉ and his
party on the twenty-first day of April last: AND to determine upon whom rests the grave responsibility of there
not having been a sufficient supply of provisions and clothing secured for the recruiting of the explorers on their
return, and for their support until they could reach the
settlements: AND generally to inquire into the organization and conduct of the Expedition: ALSO, with regard to
the claims upon the colony of the surviving members
thereof, and of the relatives (if any) of the deceased
members: Now KNOW YE that We, reposing great trust
and confidence in your integrity, knowledge, and ability,
have authorized and appointed, and by these presents do
authorize and appoint you, Sir THOMAS SIMSON PRATT, Sir
FRANCIS MURPHY, MATTHEW HERVEY, JAMES FORESTER
SULLIVAN, and EVELYN PITFIELD SHIRLEY STURT, to be
commissioners for the purpose aforesaid: AND, for the
better effecting the purpose of this Commission, we do
give and grant you power and authority to call before you
such persons as you shall judge likely to afford you any
information upon the subject of this Commission: AND to
inquire of and concerning the premises by all other lawful
means and ways whatsoever: AND this Commission shall
continue in full force and virtue, and you the said commissioners may, from time to time, and at every place or
places, proceed in the execution thereof, and of every
matter or thing therein contained, although the inquiry be
not regularly continued from time to time by adjournment: AND, LASTLY, that you do report, as occasion may
require, for the information of our Governor of our said
colony, under your hands and seals, all matters and

things elicited by you during the inquiry under this Commission.

WITNESS our trusty and well-beloved Sir HENRY BARKLY, Knight Commander of the Most Noble Order of the Bath, Captain-General and Governor-in-Chief of our colony of Victoria, and Vice-Admiral of the same, at Melbourne, this twelfth day of November, One thousand eight hundred and sixty-one, and in the twenty-fifth year of our Reign.

HENRY BARKLY.

By his Excellency's Command,
    (Signed)   R. HEALES.

REPORT.

To his Excellency Sir HENRY BARKLY, Knight Commander of the Most Honourable Order of the Bath, Captain-General and Governor-in-Chief of the colony of Victoria, and Vice-Admiral of the same, &c. &c.

MAY IT PLEASE YOUR EXCELLENCY—

In conformity with the terms of her Majesty's Commission, we have made inquiry into the circumstances connected with the sufferings and death of Robert O'Hara Burke and William John Wills, the Victorian explorers.

We have endeavoured to ascertain the true causes of
this lamentable result of the Expedition, and have
investigated the circumstances under which the
depôt at Cooper's Creek was abandoned by Mr.
William Brahé. We have sought to determine
upon whom rests the grave responsibility of there
not having been a sufficient supply of provisions
and clothing secured for the recruiting of the explorers on their return, and for their support until
they could reach the settlements ; and we have
generally inquired into the organization and conduct of the Expedition.

Our investigations have been confined to the above
matters, the Government having already taken into
consideration the claims on the colony of the surviving members of the Expedition, &c.

We have examined all persons willing to give evidence who professed, or whom we supposed to
possess, knowledge upon the various subjects of
our inquiries; and we now, after mature consideration, submit to your Excellency the following
Report :—

The Expedition, having been provided and equipped in
the most ample and liberal manner, and having reached
Menindie, on the Darling, without experiencing any difficulties, was most injudiciously divided at that point by
Mr. Burke.

It was an error of judgment on the part of Mr. Burke to
appoint Mr. Wright to an important command in the Expedition, without a previous personal knowledge of him ;
although, doubtless, a pressing urgency had arisen for the

appointment from the sudden resignations of Mr. Landells and Dr. Beckler.

Mr. Burke evinced a far greater amount of zeal than prudence in finally departing from Cooper's Creek before the depôt party had arrived from Menindie, and without having secured communication with the settled districts as he had been instructed to do ; and, in undertaking so extended a journey with an insufficient supply of provisions, Mr. Burke was forced into the necessity of overtaxing the powers of his party, whose continuous and unremitting exertions resulted in the destruction of his animals, and the prostration of himself and his companions from fatigue and severe privation.

The conduct of Mr. Wright appears to have been reprehensible in the highest degree. It is clear that Mr. Burke, on parting with him at Torowoto, relied on receiving his immediate and zealous support; and it seems extremely improbable that Mr. Wright could have misconstrued the intentions of his leader so far, as to suppose that he ever calculated for a moment on his remaining for any length of time on the Darling. Mr. Wright has failed to give any satisfactory explanation of the causes of his delay ; and to that delay are mainly attributable the whole of the disasters of the expedition, with the exception of the death of Gray. The grave responsibility of not having left a larger supply of provisions, together with some clothing, in the cache at Cooper's Creek, rests with Mr. Wright. Even had he been unable to convey stores to Cooper's Creek, he might have left them elsewhere, leaving notice at the depôt of his having done so.

The Exploration Committee, in overlooking the importance of the contents of Mr. Burke's despatch from Torowoto, and in not urging Mr. Wright's departure from the

Darling, committed errors of a serious nature.   A means of knowledge of the delay of the party at Menindie was in the possession of the Committee—not, indeed, by direct communication to that effect, but through the receipt of letters from Drs. Becker and Beckler at various dates up to the end of November, without, however, awakening the Committee to a sense of the vital importance of Mr. Burke's request in that despatch that he should " be soon followed up," or to a consideration of the disastrous consequences which would be likely to result, and did unfortunately result, from the fatal inactivity and idling of Mr. Wright and his party on the Darling.

The conduct of Mr. Brahé, in retiring from his position at the depôt before he was rejoined by his commander, or relieved from the Darling, may be deserving of considerable censure ; but we are of opinion that a responsibility far beyond his expectations devolved upon him; and it must be borne in mind that, with the assurance of his leader, and his own conviction, he might each day expect to be relieved by Mr. Wright, he still held his post for four months and five days; and that only when pressed by the appeals of a comrade sickening even to death, as was subsequently proved, his powers of endurance gave way, and he retired from the position which could alone afford succour to the weary explorers, should they return by that route.   His decision was most unfortunate; but we believe he acted from a conscientious desire to discharge his duty, and we are confident that the painful reflection that twenty-four hours' further perseverance would have made him the rescuer of the explorers, and gained for himself the praise and approbation of all, must be of itself an agonizing thought, without the addition of censure he might feel himself undeserving of.

13

It does not appear that Mr. Burke kept any regular journal, or that he gave written instructions to his officers. Had he performed these essential portions of the duties of a leader many of the calamities of the Expedition might have been averted, and little or no room would have been left for doubt in judging of the conduct of those subordinates who pleaded unsatisfactory and contradictory verbal orders and statements.

We cannot too deeply deplore the lamentable result of an expedition, undertaken at so great a cost to the colony; but, while we regret the absence of a systematic plan of operations on the part of the leader, we desire to express our admiration of his gallantry and daring, as well as of the fidelity of his brave coadjutor Mr. Wills, and their more fortunate and enduring associate, Mr. King; and we would record our feelings of deep sympathy with the deplorable sufferings and untimely deaths of Mr. Burke and his fallen comrades.

T. S. PRATT, *Chairman,*
MATTHEW HERVEY,
E. P. S. STURT,
FRANCIS MURPHY,
J. F. SULLIVAN.

Copy of a DESPATCH from Governor Sir H. BARKLY, K.C.B., to his Grace the DUKE OF NEWCASTLE, K.G.

(No. 92.)   *Government Offices, Melbourne,*
                                    November 20, 1861.

MY LORD DUKE,—The mystery in which the fate of the Victorian Exploring Expedition was shrouded when I lately alluded to it, was soon afterwards dispelled on the arrival of Mr. Brahé from the relief party, under Mr. Howitt, with intelligence that King, the sole survivor, had been found living among the natives on Cooper's Creek, his companions Burke, Wills, and Gray, having perished from exhaustion on returning from the Gulf of Carpentaria, which it now appears they reached in safety in the month of February last.

How thoroughly indeed the gallant band accomplished their perilous mission will be seen from the journals and charts of their leaders, which are fortunately preserved to us, and serve incontestably to prove, that, without detracting from the credit due to M'Donall Stuart, whose route was unknown to them and far distant from that they followed, to Burke and Wills exclusively belongs the honour of first crossing the Australian Continent from sea to sea!

The details of their discoveries, and of their sufferings, will be best learned from the simple and touching narrative which poor Wills left behind him, coupled with the statement of King, which has been taken down by Mr. Howitt ; but 1 will continue for your Grace's information the brief sketch of the history of the Expedition, begun in my Despatch of 20th July, No. 64.

I then mentioned that Mr. Burke had quitted the depôt on Cooper's Creek on the 16th December last with half his party, leaving the other half there under Mr. Brahé, whom he promoted to the rank of petty officer on the occasion, but with the expectation that the command would almost immediately be assumed by Mr. Wright, whom he had directed to join him as soon as possible with the stores left behind at the Darling ; and I described how Mr. Brahé, after waiting beyond the time Mr. Burke had anticipated being absent, and hearing nothing either of his or Wright's party, abandoned the depôt on the afternoon of the 21st

13—2

April, first burying such provisions as he could spare, after retaining enough to carry him to the Darling.

It now appears that on the evening of that very day, by a strange fatality which seems thenceforth to have prevailed to the end, Burke, Wills, and King (Gray having died four days before), reached the depôt, in far too weak and exhausted a state to follow the retreating party with the slightest hope of overtaking them, though that night they slept only fourteen miles off!

They found the food that had been left for them; and, after remaining some days to recruit, resolved, most unfortunately, instead of returning the way they had come, to try and reach the out-settlements of South Australia, not above 150 miles distant. Had they taken the route to Menindie, they would have almost immediately met Mr. Wright's advancing party, which had been delayed by causes already related.

Depositing a letter, therefore, to this effect in a bottle, which they replaced in the "cache," but again by fatal mischance neglecting to alter the inscription which Mr. Brahé had left on an adjacent tree, or to leave any outward sign of their visit, they started on a south-west course; but misfortune pursued their steps; one of the two camels which survived got bogged inextricably, and the other became so weak that they thought it best to kill it for food ; and, after wandering on till their limbs could carry them no farther, they decided to return, at a point where, though they knew it not, scarce fifty miles remained to be accomplished, and just as Mount Hopeless would have appeared above the horizon, had they continued their route for even another day.

Meanwhile, Brahé, as described in my previous despatch, revisited the depôt in company with Wright, whom he had met some days after leaving it ; but, perceiving no change, they, as a climax to this sad chapter of accidents, resumed their final journey to the Darling without opening the *cache*, or discovering the letter which Burke had substituted for theirs in the bottle !

Thus left to perish in the wilderness, the hapless explorers determined as a last resource to seek succour from the aborígines, whom they had at first viewed with suspicion. This was freely and generously afforded, so far as it was in their power to give it ; but the season was now mid-winter, the clothes of the unfortunates were in rags, and the scanty diet of fish and " nardoo " (the spores of a species of marsillea which the natives make into bread) was too unnutritious to restore frames weakened by previous over-exertion and want of nourishment, and with minds depressed by disappointment and despair, both Burke and Wills gradually sank under their privations, dying about the end of June, whilst we in Melbourne were still ignorant of the abandonment of the depôt, as well as of the obstacles which so long delayed Mr. Wright's arrival at it.

So fell two as gallant spirits as ever sacrificed life for the extension of science, or the cause of mankind ! Both were in their prime ; both resigned comfort and competency to embark in an enterprise by which they hoped to render their names glorious ; both died without a murmur, evincing their loyalty and devotion to their country to the last.

Robert O'Hara Burke, born in 1821, was the secon son of James Hardiman Burke, of St. Clerans, County Galway, an estate now possessed by the eldest son, Major Burke, late 88th Regiment. The youngest son, Lieutenant Burke, R.E., fell at the passage of the Danube in July, 1854, pierced by no less than thirty-three wounds.

Robert, like him, commenced his career as a cadet of the Woolwich Academy, but left at an early age to enter a regiment of Hungarian Hussars in the Austrian service. When this was disbanded in 1848, he obtained an appointment in the Irish Constabulary, which he, in 1853, exchanged for the police force of this colony, of which he was at once made an inspector. On the news of the Crimean war, however, he hastened home on leave of absence in hopes of getting a commission, but finding himself too late to share the glories of the campaign, returned to resume his duties here, in the discharge of which he rendered himself most popular at some of the chief gold-fields' towns. When the Exploring Expedition was resolved on, his love of adventure and thirst for distinction led him to apply for the command, and in the interval which elapsed before the Exploration Committee decided in his favour, he devoted himself with his habitual energy to qualifying himself for such a post in every possible way.

William John Wills was born at Totness, Devonshire, where his father practised medicine, in 1834, and, being destined for the same profession, entered at St. Bartholomew's, and distinguished himself, especially as student in chemistry. In 1852 the news of the gold discoveries induced him to try his fortune in this colony, and he settled at Ballarat, where he was subsequently joined by his family, and continued to assist his father for several years. His taste, however, had always been for astronomy and meteorology, and he passed all his leisure hours at the office of Mr. Taylor, the head of the Crown Lands Survey in that district, where he gave such proofs of ability as to be put in charge of a field party. Here he soon attracted the notice of the Surveyor-General, Mr. Ligar, and on the establishment of a magnetic and meteorological observatory in Melbourne, under Professor Neumayer, he was attached specially to the staff, where he remained until selected for the post of observer and surveyor to the Exploring Expedition, with which his name will ever be indelibly associated. He, too, is not the first of his family to lay down his life for his country; his cousin, Lieutenant Le Viscomte, Dr. Wills' sister's son, having accompanied Sir John Franklin in the *Erebus* on the Arctic Expedition.

Gray, it may here be added, who died of exhaustion on his way back from Carpentaria, was originally a seafaring man, whom Mr. Burke enlisted on the Darling; whilst John King, who alone lives to tell the tale, and may be expected in Melbourne shortly, was formerly a soldier, who, it is stated, came to this colony on obtaining his discharge from some regiment in India.

How far the sufferings of these devoted men arose from preventible causes, and in what degree any person or persons are to blame for the disastrous termination of a scheme, apparently so carefully devised, and which up to a certain point was eminently successful, are questions still to be determined, and regarding which I express no opinion, because a Commission has been appointed by this Government to investigate the whole matter.

The liveliest sympathy was manifested by the entire community on receipt of the glorious though disastrous news, both Houses of Parliament passing resolutions expressive of profound regret at the death of the Explorers, and of an earnest desire that every mark of respect should be shown to their memory; and it has since been settled, in pursuance of these resolutions, that Mr. Howitt shall be commissioned to send down their remains for a public funeral, and that a monument shall be erected to record an achievement, of which Victoria may well feel proud.

Apart, indeed, from the interest which must ever attach to the melancholy fate of these brave men, the results attained by the Expedition are of the very highest importance, both to geographical science, and to the progress of civilization in Australia.

The limits of the Stony Desert are proved to extend very little farther north than the point to which Sturt penetrated so many years ago, whilst the country beyond is even more adapted for settlement than that which M'Douall Stuart has discovered to the westward of it. According to the summary which poor Burke himself deposited on his return to the depôt, there is a practicable route to Carpentaria, chiefly along the 140th meridian of east longitude. " There is some good country between Cooper's Creek and the Stony Desert; from thence to the tropic all is dry and barren, but between the desert and the gulf a considerable portion, though rangy (i. e. hilly), is well watered, and richly grassed."

It has been remarked, too, by the transcriber of Wills' field-book, " that the Expedition, except when actually crossing the desert, never passed a day in which they did not traverse the banks of, or cross, a creek or other watercourse."

Such, in fact, is the impression made on the squatters by the accounts received, that the occupation of " Burke's Land " with stock is already seriously contemplated, and there seems little reason to doubt that, in the course of a few years, the journey from Melbourne to Carpentaria will be performed with comparative facility by passing from station to station. To show the rapidity with which this sort of settlement proceeds in Australia, I may mention that much of the country between the Darling and Cooper's Creek, which the several parties from Victoria have traversed, is already taken up, so that not only sheep but cattle are now depastured within twenty-five miles of Mount Bulloo, not far from which Burke's expedition struck the creek in question, stretching thence easterly along the Queensland boundary in an almost unbroken chain. To the westward, also, the country towards the South Australian settlements is likely to be occupied ere long.

I hope to be able to enclose a tracing of the entire route of the Burke and Wills Expedition, but the Surveyor-General has, of course, experienced some difficulty in connecting the various rough charts, and checking the calculations as to longitude, &c. A fuller description of some parts of the country may also be obtainable when King can be further examined, and there can be little doubt that our knowledge of the portion bordering on the Gulf of Carpentaria will be much extended by the labours of the surveyors on board her Majesty's colonial steamer *Victoria*, as well as by the party likewise despatched for the relief of Burke overland from Queensland.

It seems, indeed, not improbable, that one or other of these parties, on discovering the record left by the explorers at the mouth of the "Flinders" River (not the "Albert," as they conjectured), and supposing them never to have got back to their depôt on Cooper's Creek, may pursue their tracks to the southward until themselves are in danger; and it has been deemed advisable, in order to guard against any casualty of this sort, as well as for the purpose of connecting Burke's tropical discoveries with the depôt by the best practicable route, to instruct Mr. Howitt to establish his head-quarters for the summer there, making short excursions in every direction around, which, without exposing his men to serious risk, will be better for them than idleness or inactivity.

Some time may thus elapse before the full value and extent of these discoveries can be ascertained, but meanwhile it may be asserted, without fear of contradiction, that to the liberality and enterprise of one of her youngest colonial off-shoots, backed by the heroic self-devotion of Burke and Wills, Great Britain owes the acquisition of millions of available acres, destined at no distant day to swell her imports and afford fresh markets for her manufactures.

I have, &c.

(Signed)   HENRY BARKLY.

COPY of a DESPATCH from his Grace the DUKE of NEW-CASTLE, K.G., to Governor Sir H. BARKLY, K.C.B.

Downing Street, January 27, 1862.

SIR,—I have read with the greatest interest the intelligence conveyed in your despatch of the 20th November, respecting the fate of Mr. Burke and the adventurous persons who accompanied him on his recent disastrous expedition.

I am fully sensible of the advantages which their dearly-bought success will confer on geographical science and on their Australian fellow-colonists, and I gladly embrace this opportunity of expressing the admiration which I feel of the spirit of enterprise in which their task was undertaken, the perseverance with which it was pursued, and the patience and mutual fidelity which, even to the unhappy termination of their labours, appear never to have forsaken them.

I have, &c.

(Signed)   NEWCASTLE.

APPENDICES.

APPENDIX A.

Instructions to Leader.

Exploration Committee, Royal Society of
Victoria, Melbourne, August 18, 1860.

Sir,—I am directed by the Committee to convey to you the instructions and views which have been adopted in connection with the duties which devolve upon you as leader of the party now organized to explore the interior of Australia.

The Committee having decided upon Cooper's Creek, of Sturt's, as the basis of your operations, request that you will proceed thither, form a depôt of provisions and stores, and make arrangements for keeping open a communication in your rear to the Darling, if in your opinion advisable; and thence to Melbourne, so that you may be enabled to keep the Committee informed of your movements, and receive in return the assistance in stores and advice of which you may stand in need. Should you find that a better communication can be made by way of the South Australian Police Station, near Mount Serle, you will avail yourself of that means of writing to the Committee.

In your route to Cooper's Creek, you will avail yourself of any opportunity that may present itself for examining and reporting on the character of the country east and west of the Darling.

You will make arrangements for carrying the stores to a point opposite Mount M'Pherson, which seems to the Committee to be the best point of departure from this river for Cooper's Creek; and while the main body of the party is proceeding to that point, you may have further opportunities of examining the country on either side of your route.

In your farther progress from Mount M'Pherson towards Cooper's Creek, the Committee also desires that you should make further detours to the right and left with the same object.

The object of the Committee in directing you to Cooper's Creek is, that you should explore the country intervening between it and Leichhardt's track, south of the Gulf of Carpentaria, avoiding, as far as practicable, Sturt's route on the west, and Gregory's, down the Victoria, on the east.

To this object the Committee wishes you to devote your energies in the first instance; but should you determine the impracticability of this route, you are desired to turn westward, into the country recently discovered by Stuart, and connect his farthest point northward with Gregory's farthest Southern Exploration in 1856 (Mount Wilson).

In proceeding from Cooper's Creek to Stuart's Country, you may find the Salt Marshes an obstacle to the progress of the camels; if so, it is supposed you will be able to avoid these marshes by turning to the northward as far as Eyre's Creek, where there is permanent water, and going then westward to Stuart's farthest.

Should you, however, fail in connecting the two points of Stuart's and Gregory's farthest, or should you ascertain that this space has been already traversed, you are requested, if possible, to connect your explorations with those of the younger Gregory, in the vicinity of Mount Gould, and thence you might proceed to Sharks' Bay, or down the river Murchison to the settlements in Western Australia.

This country would afford the means of recruiting the strength of your party, and you might, after a delay of five or six months, be enabled, with the knowledge of the country you shall have previously acquired, to return by a more direct route through South Australia to Melbourne.

If you should, however, have been successful in connecting Stuart's with Gregory's farthest point in 1856 (Mount Wilson), and your party should be equal to the task, you would probably find it possible from thence to reach the country discovered by the younger Gregory.

The Committee is fully aware of the difficulty of the country you are called on traverse, and in giving you these instructions, has placed these routes before you more as an indication of what it has been deemed desirable to have accomplished than as indicating any exact course for you to pursue.

The Committee considers you will find a better and a safer guide in the natural features of the country through which you will have to pass. For all useful and practical purposes, it will be better for you and the object of future settlement that you should follow the water-courses and the country yielding herbage, than pursue any route which the Committee might be able to sketch out from an imperfect map of Australia.

The Committee intrusts you with the largest discretion as regards the forming of depôts, and your movements generally, but requests that you will mark your routes as permanently as possible, by leaving records, sowing seeds, building cairns, and marking trees at as many points as possible, consistently with your various other duties.

With reference to financial subjects, you will be furnished with a letter of authority to give orders on the treasurer for the payment of any stores or their transport, cattle, sheep, or horses you may require; and you will not fail to furnish the treasurer from time to time with detailed accounts of the articles for which you have given such orders in payment.

Each person of the party will be allowed to give authority for half of his salary being paid into any bank, or to any person he may appoint to receive the same, provided a certificate is forwarded from you to the effect that he has efficiently discharged his duty.

The Committee requests that you will make arrangements for an exact account being taken of the stores and their expenditure by the person you place in charge of them.

The Committee also requests that you would address all your communications on subjects connected with the exploration to the Honorary Secretary; and that all persons acting with you should forward their communications on the same subject through you.

You will cause full reports to be furnished by your officers on any subject of interest, and forward them to Melbourne as often as may be practicable without retarding the progress of the Expedition.

The Committee has caused the inclosed set of instructions to be drawn up having relation to each department of science, and you are requested to hand each of the gentlemen a copy of the part more particularly relating to his department.

> I have the honour to be, sir,
>> Your most obedient servant,
>>> (Signed)   John Macadam, M.D.,
>>>> *Honorary Secretary, E.C., R.S.V.*

Robert O'Hara Burke, Esq.,
    Leader, Victorian Exploring Expedition.

APPENDIX B.

King's Narrative.

Mr. Burke, Mr. Wills, and I reached the depôt at Cooper's Creek on April 21st, about half-past seven in the evening, with two camels—all that remained of the six Mr. Burke took with him. All the provisions we then had consisted of a pound and a half of dried meat. We found the party had gone the same day, and looking about for any mark they might have left, found the tree with "DIG, April 21." Mr. Wills said the party had left for the Darling. We dug, and found the plant of stores. Mr. Burke took the papers out of the bottle, and then asked each of us whether we were able to proceed up the creek in pursuit of the party. We said not; and he then said that he thought it his duty to ask us, but that he himself was unable to do so; but that he had decided upon trying to make Mount Hopeless, as he had been assured by the Committee in Melbourne that there was a cattle station within one hundred and fifty

miles of Cooper's Creek. Mr. Wills was not inclined to
follow this plan, but wished to go down our old track; but
at last gave in to Mr. Burke's wishes. I also wished to go
down by our old track. We remained four or five days to
recruit, and make preparations to go down the creek by
stages of four to five miles a day; and Mr. Burke placed a
paper in the plant, stating what were our plans. Travelling
down the creek, we got some fish from the natives, and,
some distance down, one of the camels (Linda) got bogged;
and although we remained there that day and part of the
next trying to dig him out, we found our strength
insufficient to do so. The evening of the second day we
shot him as he lay; and having cut off as much meat as
we could, we lived on it while we stayed to dry the
remainder. Throwing all the least necessary things away,
we made one load for the remaining camel (Rajah), and
each of us carried a swag of about 25lbs. We were then
tracing down the branches of the creek running S., but
found that they ran out into earthy plains. We had
understood that the creek along Gregory's track was
continuous; and finding that all these creeks ran out into
plains, Mr. Burke returned, our camel being completely
knocked up. We then intended to give the camel a spell
for a few days, and to make a new attempt to push on
forty or fifty miles to the south, in the hope of striking the
creek. During the time that the camel was being rested,
Mr. Burke and Mr. Wills went in search of the natives, to
endeavour to find out how the nardoo grew. Having found
their camp, they obtained as much nardoo cake and fish
as they could eat, but could not explain that they wished
to be shown how to find the seed themselves. They
returned on the third day, bringing some fish and nardoo
cake with them. On the following day the camel Rajah

seemed very ill, and I told Mr. Burke I thought he could not linger out more than four days; and as on the same evening the poor brute was on the point of dying, Mr. Burke ordered him to be shot. I did so, and we cut him up with two broken knives and a lancet. We cured the meat and planted it; and Mr. Burke then made another attempt to find the nardoo, taking me with him. We went down the creek, expecting to find the natives at the camp where they had been last seen, but found that they had left; and not knowing whether they were gone up or down the creek, we slept in their gunyahs that night, and on the following morning returned to Mr. Wills. The next day Mr. Burke and I started up the creek, but could see nothing of them; and were three days away when we returned, and remained three days in our camp with Mr. Wills. We then made a plant of all the articles we could not carry with us, leaving 5lbs. of rice and a quantity of meat, and then followed up the creek, where there were some good native huts. We remained at that place a few days; and finding our provisions were beginning to run short, Mr. Burke said that we ought to do something, and that if we did not find the nardoo we should starve, and that he intended to save a little dried meat and rice to carry us to Mount Hopeless. The three of us then came to the conclusion that it would be better to make a second attempt to reach Mount Hopeless, as we were then as strong as we were likely to be, our daily allowance being then reduced. Mr. Burke asked each of us whether we were willing to make another attempt to reach the South Australian settlements, and we decided on going. We took with us what remained of the provisions we had planted—two-and-a-half pounds of oatmeal, a small quantity of flour, and the dried meat—this, with powder

and shot, and other small articles, made up our swags to
30lbs. each, and Mr. Burke carried one billy of water, and I
another. We had not gone far before we came on a flat, where
I saw a plant growing which I took to be clover, and on looking closer, saw the seed, and called out that I had found the
nardoo. They were very glad when I found it. We travelled
three days, and struck a watercourse coming south from
Cooper's Creek. We traced this, as it branched out and
re-formed on the plains, until we at last lost it in flat country.
Sand-hills were in front of us, for which we made, and travelled all day, but found no water. We were all greatly
fatigued, as our rations now consisted of only one small johnny
cake and three sticks of dried meat daily. We camped that
evening about four o'clock, intending to push next day
until two o'clock P.M., and then, should we not find water,
to return. We travelled, and found no water, and the
three of us sat down and rested for an hour, and then
turned back. We all felt satisfied that, had there been a
few days' rain, we could have got through. We were
then, according to Mr. Wills' calculation, forty-five miles
from the creek. We travelled on the day we turned back
very late, and the following evening reached the nearest
water at the creek. We gathered some nardoo, and
boiled the seeds, as we were unable to pound them. The
following day we reached the main creek; and knowing
where there was a fine water-hole and native gunyahs, we
went there, intending to save what remained of our flour
and dried meat, for the purpose of making another attempt
to reach Mount Hopeless. On the following day Mr.
Wills and I went out to gather nardoo, of which we
obtained a supply sufficient for three days; and finding a
pounding-stone at the gunyahs, Mr. Wills and I pounded
the seed, which was such slow work that we were com-

pelled to use half flour and half nardoo. Mr. Burke and
Mr. Wills then went down the creek for the remainder of
the dried meat which we had planted; and we had now all
our things with us, gathering nardoo, and living the best
way we could. Mr. Burke requested Mr. Wills to go up
the creek as far as the depôt, and to place a note in the
plant there, stating that we were then living on the creek,
the former note having stated that we were on our road to
South Australia. He was also to bury there the field-books
of the journey to the Gulf. Before starting he got 3lbs. of
flour and 3lbs. of pounded nardoo, and about a pound of
meat, as he expected to be absent about eight days.
During his absence I gathered nardoo and pounded it, as
Mr. Burke wished to lay in a supply, in case of rain.

A few days after Mr. Wills left, some natives came down
to the creek, to fish at some water-holes near our camp.
They were civil to us at first, and offered us some fish; on
the second day they came again to fish, and Mr. Burke
took down two bags, which they filled for him; on the
third they gave us one bag of fish, and afterwards all came
to our camp. We used to keep our ammunition and other
articles in one gunyah, and all three of us lived together
in another. One of the natives took an oilcloth out of this
gunyah; and Mr. Burke seeing him run away with it,
followed him with his revolver and fired over his head,
and upon this the native dropped the oilcloth. While he
was away the other blacks invited me away to a water-hole
to eat fish ; but I declined to do so, as Mr. Burke was
away, and a number of natives were about who would
have taken all our things. When I refused, one took his
boomerang and laid it over my shoulder, and then told me
by signs that if I called out for Mr. Burke, as I was doing,
that he would strike me. Upon this I got them all in front

of the gunyah, and fired a revolver over their heads; but they did not seem at all afraid, until I got out the gun, when they all ran away. Mr. Burke, hearing the report, came back, and we saw no more of them until late that night, when they came with some cooked fish, and called out "White fellow." Mr. Burke then went out with his revolver, and found a whole tribe coming down, all painted, and with fish in small nets carried by two men. Mr. Burke went to meet them, and they wished to surround him; but he knocked as many of the nets of fish out of their hands as he could, and shouted out to me to fire. I did so, and they ran off. We collected five small nets of cooked fish. The reason he would not accept the fish from them was, that he was afraid of being too friendly, lest they should be always at our camp. We then lived on fish until Mr. Wills returned. He told us that he had met the natives soon after leaving us, and that they were very kind to him and had given him plenty to eat both on going up and returning. He seemed to consider that he should have very little difficulty in living with them; and as our camp was close to theirs, he returned to them the same day and found them very hospitable and friendly, keeping him with them two days. They then made signs to him to be off. He came to us and narrated what had happened, but went back to them the following day, when they gave him his breakfast, but made signs to him to go away. He pretended not to understand them, and would not go; upon which they made signs that they were going up the creek, and that he had better go down. They packed up and left the camp, giving Mr. Wills a little nardoo to take to us.

During his absence, while Mr. Burke was cooking some fish, during a strong wind, the flames caught the gunyah, and burned so rapidly that we were unable, not only to put it out, but to save any of our things, excepting one revolver and a gun. Mr. Wills being returned, it was decided to go up the creek and live with the natives, if possible, as Mr. Wills thought we should have but little difficulty in obtaining provisions from them if we camped on the opposite side of the creek to them. He said he knew where they were gone, so we packed up and started. Coming to the gunyahs where we expected to have found them, we were disappointed, and seeing a nardoo field close by, halted, intending to make it our camp. For some time we were employed gathering nardoo, and laying up a supply. Mr. Wills and I used to collect and carry home a bag each day, and Mr. Burke generally pounded sufficient for our dinner during our absence; but Mr. Wills found himself getting very weak, and was shortly unable to go out and gather nardoo as before, nor even strong enough to pound it; so that in a few days he became almost helpless. I still continued gathering; and Mr. Burke now also began to feel very weak, and said he could be of very little use in pounding. I had now to gather and pound for all three of us. I continued to do this for a few days, but finding my strength rapidly failing, my legs being very weak and painful, I was unable to go out for several days, and we were compelled to consume six days' stock, which we had laid by. Mr. Burke now proposed that I should gather as much as possible in three days, and that with this supply we should go in search of the natives— a plan which had been urged upon us by Mr. Wills as the only chance of saving him and ourselves as well, as he clearly saw that I was no longer able to collect sufficient for our wants. Having collected the seed, as proposed, and having pounded sufficient to last Mr. Wills for eight days, and two days for ourselves, we placed water and fire-wood within his reach, and started. Before leaving him, however, Mr. Burke asked him whether he still wished it, as under no other circumstances would he leave him ; and Mr. Wills again said that he looked on it as our only chance. He then gave Mr. Burke a letter and his watch for his father, and we buried the remainder of his field-books near the gunyah. Mr. Wills said that, in case of my surviving Mr. Burke, he hoped that I would carry out his last wishes in giving the watch and letter to his father.

In travelling the first day, Mr. Burke seemed very weak, and complained of great pain in his legs and back. On the second day he seemed to be better, and said that he thought he was getting stronger; but, on starting, did not go two miles before he said he could go no farther. I persisted in his trying to go on, and managed to get him along several times, until I saw that he was almost knocked up, when he said he could not carry his swag, and threw all he had away. I also reduced mine, taking nothing but a gun and some powder and shot, and a small pouch and some matches. On starting again, we did not go far before Mr. Burke said he should halt for the night; but, as the place was close to a large sheet of water, and exposed to the wind, I prevailed on him to go a little farther, to the next reach of water, where we camped. We searched about, and found a few small patches of nardoo, which I collected and pounded, and, with a crow which I shot, made a good evening's meal. From the time we halted Mr. Burke seemed to be getting worse, although he ate his supper. He said he felt convinced he could not last many hours, and gave me his watch, which he said belonged to the Committee, and a pocket-book to give to Sir William

Stawell, and in which he wrote some notes. He then said to me, " I hope you will remain with me here till I am quite dead ; it is a comfort to know that some one is by ; but when I am dying, it is my wish that you should place the pistol in my right hand, and that you leave me unburied as I lie." That night he spoke very little, and the following morning I found him speechless, or nearly so ; and about eight o'clock he expired. I remained a few hours there, but as I saw there was no use in remaining longer, I went up the creek in search of the natives. I felt very lonely, and at night usually slept in deserted wurleys, belonging to the natives. Two days after leaving the spot where Mr. Burke died, I found some gunyahs, where the natives had deposited a bag of nardoo, sufficient to last me a fortnight, and three bundles containing various articles. I also shot a crow that evening, but was in very great dread that the natives would come and deprive me of the nardoo.

I remained there two days to recover my strength, and then returned to Mr. Wills. I took back three crows, but found him lying dead in his gunyah, and the natives had been there and had taken away some of his clothes. I buried the corpse with sand, and remained there some days. But finding that my stock of nardoo was running short, and being unable to gather it, I tracked the natives who had been to the camp, by their footprints in the sand ; and, when some distance down the creek, shooting crows and hawks on the road, the natives, hearing the report of the gun, came to meet me, and took me with them to their camp, giving me nardoo and fish. They took the birds I had shot and cooked them for me, and afterwards showed me a gunyah, where I was to sleep with three of the single men. The following morning they commenced talking to me, and putting one finger on the ground, and covering it with sand, at the same time pointing up the creek, saying, " White fellow," which I understood to mean that one white man was dead. From this I thought they were the tribe who had taken Mr. Wills' clothes. They then asked me where the third man was, and I also made the sign of putting the fingers on the ground, and covering them with sand, at the same time pointing up the creek. They appeared to feel great compassion for me when they understood that I was alone on the creek, and gave me plenty to eat. After being four days with them, I saw that they were becoming tired of me, and they made signs that they were going up the creek, and that I had better go downwards; but I pretended not to understand them. The same day they shifted camp, and I followed them; and, on reaching their camp, I shot some crows, which pleased them so much that they made me a breakwind in the centre of their camp, and came and sat round me until such time as the crows were cooked, when they assisted me to eat them. The same day, one of the women, to whom I had given part of a crow, came and gave me a ball of nardoo, saying that she would give me more only she had such a sore arm that she was unable to pound. She showed me a sore on her arm, and the thought struck me that I would boil some water in the billy and wash her arm with a sponge. During the operation the whole tribe sat round, and were muttering one to another. Her husband sat down by her side, and she was crying all the time. After I had washed it, I touched it with some nitrate of silver, when she began to yell and ran off, crying, " Mokow! mokow!" (fire! fire!) From this time she and her husband used to give me a small quantity of nardoo both night and morning, and whenever the tribe was about going on a fishing excursion he used to give me notice to go with them. They also used to assist me in making a wurley or breakwind whenever they shifted camp. I generally shot a crow, or a hawk, and gave it to them in return for these little services. Every four or five days the tribe would surround me and ask whether I intended going up or down the creek. At last I made them understand that if they went up I should go up the creek, and if they went down I should also go down; and from this time they seemed to look upon me as one of themselves, and supplied me with fish and nardoo regularly. They were very anxious, however, to know where Mr. Burke lay; and one day, when we were fishing in the water-holes close by, I took them to the spot. On seeing his remains, the whole party wept bitterly, and covered them with bushes. After this they were much kinder to me than before, and I always told them that the white men would be here before two moons; and in the evenings, when they came with nardoo and fish, they used to talk about the "white fellows" coming, and the same time pointing to the moon. I also told them they would receive many presents, and they constantly asked me for toma-hawks, called by them "bomayho." From this time to when the relief party arrived, a period of about a month, they treated me with uniform kindness, and looked upon me as one of themselves. The day on which I was re-leased, one of the tribe who had been fishing came and told me that the "white fellows" were coming; and the whole of the tribe, who were then in camp, sallied out in every direction to meet the party, while the man who had brought the news took me over the creek, where I shortly saw the party coming down.

APPENDIX C.

Mr. Burke's Notes of the Expedition.

These notes were often illegible, and in many places the pages of the book had been ripped and cut out. The book was evidently kept for rough memoranda.

The following extracts are from the memorandum book of Mr. Burke. Mr. Archer, to whom the task of transcribing it was intrusted, writes the following preface:—" I went carefully through Burke's note-book last night. It is an ordinary memorandum book, with a clasp, and a side pocket for a pencil. It is much dilapidated, and several of the leaves are torn out ; some so torn had been written on. I have numbered these consecutively throughout. The following is a copy, letter for letter, and word for word, of all that remains of Burke's pencillings. I have queried all doubtful points : "—

No. 69. line of cour i ing on bags 1, 4, 19, 20, 11, 3. Think well before giving an answer, and never speak except from strong convictions.

16th December.—Left Depôt 65, followed by the creek.

17th.—The same ; 66.

18th.—The same ; 67.

19th.—We made a (?) small creek, supposed to be Otto Era (?), or in the immediate neighbourhood of it. Good water. Camp 69.

20th.—Made a creek, where we found a great many natives : they presented us with fish, and offered their women. Camp 70.

21st.—Made another creek ; Camp 71. Splendid water ; fine feed for the camels ; would be a very good place for a station. Since we have left Cooper's Creek we have travelled over a very fine sheep-grazing country, well watered, and in every respect well suited for occupation.

22nd December, 1860.—Camp 72. Encamped on the borders of the desert.

23rd.—Travelled day and night, and encamped in the night in the bed of a creek, as we supposed we were near water.

24th.—Encamped on the morning of this day on the banks of Gray's Creek, called after him because he was detached on horseback from the party, and found it good water. The third day without it. Now for a retrospective glance. We started from Cooper's Creek, Camp 66, with the intention of going through to Eyre's Creek without water. Loaded with 800 pints of water, four riding camels carried 130 pints, each horse 150, two pack camels 50 each, and five pints each man.

25th (Christmas Day).—Started at four A.M. from Gray's Creek, and arrived at a creek which appears to be quite as large as Cooper's Creek. At two P.M. Golah Sing gave some very decided hints about stopping by lying down under the trees. Splendid prospect.

26th December, 27th December, 28th December, 29th December.—Followed up the creek until it took a turn to the south-east, which I thought rather too much to put up with, therefore left it on the morning of the 30th December; 12.30, on the road. Started at seven o'clock; travelled eleven hours.

31st.—Started at 2.20; 16½ hours on the road. Travelled 13½ hours.

1st January.—Water.

2d January.—From King's Creek; 11 hours on the

road. Started at seven; travelled nine and a half hours. Desert.

3d. January.—Five started. Travelled 12 hours, no minutes.

4th.—Twelve hours on the road.

5th. Water at Wills' or King's Creek. It is impossible to say the time we were up, for we had to load the camels, to pack and feed them, to watch them and the horse, and to look for water; but I am satisfied that the frame of man never was more severely taxed.

Here follows an entry for March 28th, commencing thus : "March 28th—At the conclusion of—" then some of the leaves appear to have been torn out from pages 43 to 55.

13th January, 1861.—As I find it impossible to keep a regular diary, I shall jot down my ideas when I have an opportunity, and put the date. Upon two occasions, at Cooper's Creek and at King's Creek, on New Year's Day, whenever the natives tried to bully or bounce us, and were repulsed, although the leaders appeared to be in earnest, the followers, and particularly the young ones, laughed heartily, and seemed to be amused at their leaders' repulse. The old fellow at King's Creek, who stuck his spear into the ground, and threw dust in the air, when I fired off my pistol, ran off in the most undignified manner. Names for places : Thackeray, Barry, Bindon, Lyons, Forbes, Archer, Bennet, Colles, O. S. Nicholson, Wood, Wrixon, Cope, Turner, Scratchley, Ligar, Griffith, Green, Roe, Hamilton, Archer, Colles.

18th January.—Still on the ranges; the camels sweating profusely from fear.

20th January.—I determined to-day to go straight at the ranges, and so far the experiment has succeeded well.

The poor camels sweating and groaning, but we gave them a hot bath in Turner's Creek, which seemed to relieve them very much. At last through—the camels bleeding, sweating, and groaning. [Leaves 35 to 39 torn out, and eight leaves preceding torn out; no marks of writing visible on the remnant. Leaves 24 to 33, both inclusive, blank on both sides.]

28th March.—At the conclusion of report, it would be well to say that we reached the sea, but we could not obtain a view of the open ocean, although we made every endeavour to do so.

Leaving Carpentaria :—flour 83 lb., pork 3 lb., d. meat 35 lb., biscuits 12 lb., rice 12 lb., sugar 10 lb. [Page 15 blank.] Return party from Carpentaria arrived here last night, and found that the D. party had started on the same day. We proceed slowly down the creek, towards Adelaide, by Mount Hopeless, and shall endeavour to follow Gregory's track; but we are very weak, the camels are done up, and we shall not be able to travel faster than five miles a day at most. Gray died on the road from hunger and fatigue. We all suffered much from hunger, but the provisions left here will, I think, restore our strength. We have discovered a practicable route to Carpentaria, the principal portion of which lies in the 140th meridian of east longitude. Between this and the Stony Desert there is some good country; from there to the tropic, the country is dry and stony; between the tropic and Carpentaria a considerable portion is rangy, but it is well watered and richly grassed.

Pages 20 and 21 torn ; no writing apparent.

Pages 22 and 23 contain a memorandum of stores, but without any particular reference to time and place.

APPENDIX D.

Copy of a Letter from the Colonial Office to Major Burke, 3rd Regiment.

Downing Street, January 30, 1862.

Sir,—I am directed by the Duke of Newcastle to transmit to you a copy of a despatch from the Governor of Victoria, in which he reports the melancholy death of your brother, Mr. Robert Burke, and, with one exception, of his companions, on their return to the Colony, after accomplishing the object of their Exploring Expedition.

The Duke of Newcastle has desired me to express to you, with what concern he has received this intelligence, and to assure you of his admiration of the noble efforts made by your brother to perform the arduous duty confided to his charge.

I am, sir,
Your obedient servant,

Major Burke.   (Signed)   Frederick Rogers.

APPENDIX E.

Extracts from a Letter from Sir Henry Barkly, K.C.B., Governor of Victoria, to Major Burke, 3rd Regiment.

Government House, Melbourne,
November 25, 1861.

Sir,—As your brother, Mr. Robert O'Hara Burke, was on leave of absence from the service of this Government at the time of his lamented decease, as leader of the

Exploring Expedition, by which the continent of Australia has first been crossed from sea to sea, I consider it my duty to communicate to you the particulars of the sad event, as well as of the honours that are about to be paid to his memory.

* * * * *

The liveliest sympathy was felt by the entire community on the receipt of the news. . . . . Both Houses of Parliament passed resolutions expressive of grief for the sufferings and death of the gallant explorers, and of their desire to do honour to their memory, by giving their remains, which will be brought down for the purpose, a public funeral, and erecting a monument over their tomb, for which two thousand pounds have been already appropriated.

This colony, indeed, may well be proud, not merely that such an achievement has been performed, but of the heroism and self-devotion exhibited in its performance; and I am sure that when the simple narrative of the explorers comes to be read in the mother country, it will be felt that Ireland never sent out a truer or a braver son than Robert O'Hara Burke, of whom you, as the head and representative of the family, will, I doubt not, hold as high account, as any of its gallant members who have fallen in the service of their Queen and country.

I have, &c.

(Signed)   HENRY BARKLY,

Governor of Victoria.

15

APPENDIX F.

EXTRACT from a RESOLUTION passed by the GRAND JURY of the County of Galway.

Galway Spring Assizes, 1862.

Resolved—That this the Grand Inquest of his native county do not deem it right to separate without recording their high appreciation of the devoted heroism in Australia of the late lamented Robert O'Hara Burke.

One brother has already gone down to posterity as the hero of Silistria.*

Another has now solved the geographical problem of the interior of Australia, and his name must be ever associated with the vast district of Carpentaria.

And we trust that Parliament will duly appreciate such important and distinguished service. . . . .

(Signed)   C. J. O'KELLY, *Foreman.*

APPENDIX G.

EXTRACT from Proceedings of the ANNUAL MEETING of the ROYAL GEOGRAPHICAL SOCIETY, held at London, on Monday the 26th May, 1862.†

Lord ASHBURTON said, before he proceeded to award the medals, he might be allowed to say that they were not the gift of a set of private gentlemen, but that the Crown had

* Query Giurgevo?
† From the *Times* of 27th May, 1862.

selected the President and Fellows of the Royal Geographical Society to present the honours to those who had most distinguished themselves in the pursuit of geographical science. They had always been given with the strictest impartiality, and quite independent of any political bias. The noble lord then handed to the Duke of Newcastle the founder's gold medal, to be transmitted by him to the representative of the late Robert O'Hara Burke. (Cheers.)

The Duke of NEWCASTLE, who was received with loud applause, said he assured the meeting that he attended there in fulfilment of what he considered a public duty, at once painful and agreeable—painful because he received at the hands of the President this token of admiration of one of England's great men, for transmission not to him for whose merits it had been bestowed, and who was now cold on the shores of that great country on which he had conferred such great benefits, but to those relatives who, like the colony itself, must look back upon his memory with affectionate admiration. At the same time, it was a pleasurable duty, because it showed that this society, as well as the country at large, had not been insensible to the merits of the individual or the services he had rendered to science and civilization. These medals, as it had been correctly stated by the chairman, were not conferred at the option of private individuals, but by the Crown, through the instrumentality of the President and Fellows of that society; but the medals must bear an additional value when it was recollected that they were not bestowed upon any arbitrary principles, but by gentlemen eminent for their knowledge and experience, and who were well calculated to appreciate the merit they rewarded. Standing before them as he did, intrusted by her Majesty with the seals of the Colonial Office, he felt bound to express his admiration of the colony of Victoria in instituting this Expedition.   That was perhaps the one of the Australian colonies least interested in the result of Mr. Burke's expedition; at the same time it entered upon it with that public spirit which had actuated this country in similar expeditions—a desire to benefit science and to extend civilization throughout Australia, of which the colony of Victoria formed so important a part.   (Hear, hear.)   But if credit was due to Victoria for this, it was also due to that colony to acknowledge that it set on foot other expeditions when the fate of Mr. Burke was held in the balance, and when it was hoped that expeditions might afford aid or probably effect his rescue.   It would be unnecessary to say much upon the individual merits of Mr. Burke, for most of those present had read that touching despatch of Sir Henry Barkly in which he narrated the circumstances of Mr. Burke's untimely fate.   In him they had lost a man as eminent, as gallant, and as great as that intrepid brother who perished on the banks of the Danube.   (Cheers.)   He felt certain that the society had done well in awarding its medal to so distinguished an explorer.   It would not be proper for him to pledge the Colonial Office to anything on such an occasion, but he would say that on all such matters as that the authorities of that office looked to the Royal Geographical Society as a guide and instructor, and, although it might not be always possible to follow what was suggested, it would always be with great deference that they received suggestions, and with great reluctance that they were unable to carry them out.   On the part of the friends of Mr. Burke he thanked the society, and assured them that the medal should be duly transmitted to them. (Hear.)

Lord ASHBURTON then presented to his Grace the gold watch which had been awarded to Mr. King, the sole survivor of the Expedition under Burke.

The Duke of NEWCASTLE said he should feel the greatest pleasure in transmitting the watch to King, who, he believed, was in the colony. The Marseilles mail would leave that day, and he would send it at once. Although King was not a leading spirit in the Expedition, they owed much to him, and if he had not survived, they would have received but little of the valuable information they now possessed.

Sir R. MURCHISON was happy to announce that the Governor and Legislature of Victoria had granted to King a comfortable annuity for life. (Cheers.)

Lord ASHBURTON read a paper on the progress of geographical science, and Sir R. MURCHISON, in the course of a paper on Australia suggested that that portion which had been explored by Mr. Burke should be hereafter called Burke's Land. (Cheers.)

THE END.

LONDON:
PRINTED BY SMITH, ELDER AND CO.,
LITTLE GREEN ARBOUR COURT, OLD BAILEY, E.C.

65, *Cornhill, London,*
September, 1862.

NEW AND STANDARD WORKS

PUBLISHED BY

SMITH, ELDER AND CO.

Journal of a Political Mission to Afghanistan,

With an Account of the Country and People.
By H. W. Bellew, Medical Officer to the Mission.
With 8 Plates. Demy 8vo.

Robert O'Hara Burke and the Australian

Exploring Expedition of 1860.
By Andrew Jackson.
With Map and Portrait. Post 8vo.

Our Last Years in India.

By Mrs. John B. Speid.
Post 8vo. Price 9s. cloth.

Against Wind and Tide.

By Holme Lee.
Author of "Sylvan Holt's Daughter," "Kathie Brande," &c. A New and
Cheaper Edition. Fcap 8vo. Price 2s. 6d. cloth.

Reminiscences of Captain Gronow,

Formerly of the Grenadier Guards, and M.P. for Stafford.
Being Anecdotes of the Camp, the Court, and the Clubs,
at the close of the Last War with France.
Related by Himself. With Four Illustrations. Second Edition, Revised.
Crown 8vo. 9s. cloth.

Vancouver Island and British Columbia:

Where they are; What they are; and What they may
become. A Sketch of their History, Topography, Climate,
Resources, Capabilities, and Advantages, especially as Colo-
nies for Settlement.
By Dr. Alexander Rattray, of the Royal Navy.
Post 8vo. 4 Plates and 2 Maps. 5s. cloth.

The Adventures of Philip on his Way through

the World; shewing who Robbed him, who Helped him,
and who Passed him by.
By W. M. Thackeray,
Author of "Esmond," "Vanity Fair," "Virginians," &c.
Three Volumes. Post 8vo.

Essays by a Barrister.
(Reprinted from the *Saturday Review*.)
Post 8vo. Price 9s. cloth.

The Rifle in Cashmere.
A Narrative of Shooting Expeditions in Ladak, Cashmere, &c.
With Advice on Travelling, Shooting, and Stalking. To which are
added notes on Army Reform and Indian Politics.
By Arthur Brinckman, Late of H.M.'s 94th Regiment.
With Two Illustrations. Post 8vo. Price 8s. 6d. cloth.

Life in the Forests of the Far East.
By Spenser St. John, F.R.G.S., F.E.S.
Late H.M.'s Consul-General in Borneo, now H.M.'s Chargé d'Affaires to Hayti.
Illustrated with Sixteen Coloured and Tinted Lithographs, and Three
Maps. Two Volumes. Demy 8vo. Price 32s.

Studies in Animal Life.
By George Henry Lewes.
Author of "The Life of Goethe," "Sea Side Studies," "Physiology of
Common Life," &c. With Illustrations. Post 8vo. Price 5s. cloth.

NEW NOVELS.

Normanton.
By A. J. Barrowcliffe. Author of "Amberhill," and "Trust for Trust."
One Vol.

Winifred's Wooing.
By Georgiana M. Craik, Author of "Lost and Won," &c. In One Vol.

Intellectual Education, and its Influence on
the Character and Happiness of Women.
By Emily Shirreff. Second Edition. Crown 8vo. Price 6s. cloth.

Flowers for Ornament and Decoration;
and How to Arrange Them.
By E. A. Maling.
With Coloured Frontispiece. Price 2s. 6d. cloth.

By the same Author.

In-door Plants; and How to Grow Them for
the Drawing-Room, Balcony, and Green-House.
5th Thousand. With Coloured Frontispiece. Price 2s. 6d. cloth.

Song Birds; and How to Keep Them.
With Coloured Frontispiece. Fcap 8vo. Price 2s. 6d. cloth.

HISTORY AND BIOGRAPHY.

History of the Four Conquests of England.
By James Augustus St. John, Esq.
Two Vols. 8vo. Price 28*s.* cloth.

History of the Venetian Republic:
By W. Carew Hazlitt.
Complete in 4 vols. 8vo, with Illustrations, price 2*l.* 16*s.*, cloth.
*** Volumes III. and IV. may be had separately.

The Life and Letters of Captain John Brown.
Edited by Richard D. Webb.
With Portrait. Fcap 8vo. Price 4*s.* 6*d.* cloth.

Life of Schleiermacher,
As unfolded in his Autobiography and Letters.
Translated by Frederica Rowan.
Two vols. post 8vo, with Portrait. Price One Guinea, cloth.

The Life of Charlotte Brontë (Currer Bell).
By Mrs. Gaskell.
Fourth Library Edition, revised, one vol., with a Portrait of Miss Brontë and a View of Haworth Parsonage. Price 7*s.* 6*d.*; morocco elegant, 14*s.*

Life of Edmond Malone,
Editor of Shakspeare's Works. With Selections from his MS. Anecdotes.
By Sir James Prior.
Demy 8vo, with Portrait, 14*s.* cloth.

The Autobiography of Leigh Hunt.
One vol., post 8vo, with Portrait. Library edition. Price 7*s.* 6*d.* cloth.

Life of Lord Metcalfe.
By John William Kaye.
New Edition, in Two Vols., post 8vo, with Portrait. Price 12*s.* cloth.

Life of Sir John Malcolm, G.C.B.
By John William Kaye.
Two Vols. 8vo, with Portrait. Price 36*s.* cloth.

The Autobiography of Lutfullah.
A Mohamedan Gentleman; with an Account of his Visit to England.
Edited by E. B. Eastwick, Esq.
Third Edition, Fcap 8vo. Price 5*s.* cloth.

The Life of Mahomet.
With Introductory Chapters on the Original Sources for the Biography of Mahomet, and on the Pre-Islamite History of Arabia.
By W. Muir, Esq., Bengal C.S.
Complete in Four Vols. Demy 8vo. Price 2*l.* 2*s.* cloth.
*** Vols. III. and IV. may be had separately, price 21*s.*

Robert Owen and his Social Philosophy.
By William Lucas Sargant.
1 vol., post 8vo. 10*s.* 6*d.* cloth.

Women of Christianity
Exemplary for Piety and Charity.
By Julia Kavanagh.
Post 8vo, with Portraits. Price 5*s.* in embossed cloth.

VOYAGES AND TRAVELS.

Scripture Lands

In connection with their History:

With an Appendix: and Extracts from a Journal kept during an Eastern Tour in 1856-7.

By the Rev. G. S. Drew,

Author of "Scripture Studies," &c. Second Edition, post 8vo, with a Map, price 10s. 6d. cloth.

A Visit to the Philippine Isles in 1858–59.

By Sir John Bowring,

Demy 8vo, with numerous Illustrations, price 18s. cloth.

Heathen and Holy Lands;

Or, Sunny Days on the Salween, Nile, and Jordan.

By Captain J. P. Briggs, Bengal Army.

Post 8vo, price 12s. cloth.

Narrative of the Mission to Ava.

By Captain Henry Yule, Bengal Engineers.

Imperial 8vo, with Twenty-four Plates (Twelve coloured), Fifty Woodcuts, and Four Maps. Elegantly bound in cloth, with gilt edges, price 2l. 12s. 6d.

Egypt in its Biblical Relations.

By the Rev. J. Foulkes Jones.

Post 8vo, price 7s. 6d. cloth.

Japan, the Amoor, and the Pacific.

A Voyage of Circumnavigation in the Imperial Russian Corvette "Rynda," in 1858-59-60.

By Henry Arthur Tilley.

8vo, with illustrations, 16s. cloth.

Through Norway with a Knapsack.

By W. M. Williams.

With Six Coloured Views. Third Edition, post 8vo, price 12s. cloth.

Turkish Life and Character.

By Walter Thornbury.

Author of "Life in Spain," &c. &c. Two Vols., with Eight Tinted Illustrations, price 21s. cloth.

Voyage to Japan,

Kamtschatka, Siberia, Tartary, and the Coast of China, in H.M.S. *Barracouta.*

By J. M. Tronson, R.N.

8vo, with Charts and Views. 18s. cloth.

To Cuba and Back.

By R. H. Dana,

Author of "Two Years before the Mast," &c.

Post 8vo, price 7s. cloth.

Life and Liberty in America.

By Dr. C. Mackay.

Second Edition, 2 vols., post 8vo, with Ten Tinted Illustrations, price 21s.

WORKS OF MR. RUSKIN.

Modern Painters.

Now complete in five vols., Imperial 8vo, with 87 Engravings on Steel, and 216 on Wood, chiefly from Drawings by the Author. With Index to the whole Work.   Price 8*l.* 6*s.* 6*d.*, in cloth.

EACH VOLUME MAY BE HAD SEPARATELY.

Vol. I.   6th Edition.   OF GENERAL PRINCIPLES AND OF TRUTH. Price 18*s.* cloth.

Vol. II.   4th Edition.   OF THE IMAGINATIVE AND THEORETIC FACULTIES.   Price 10*s.* 6*d.* cloth.

Vol. III. OF MANY THINGS. With Eighteen Illustrations drawn by the Author, and engraved on Steel. Price 38*s.* cloth.

Vol. IV. ON MOUNTAIN BEAUTY. With Thirty-five Illustrations engraved on Steel, and 116 Woodcuts, drawn by the Author. Price 2*l.* 10*s.* cloth.

Vol. V.   OF LEAF BEAUTY; OF CLOUD BEAUTY; OF IDEAS OF RELATION. With Thirty-four Engravings on Steel, and 100 on Wood.   Price 2*l.* 10*s.* With Index to the five volumes.

The Stones of Venice.

Complete in Three Volumes, Imperial 8vo, with Fifty-three Plates and numerous Woodcuts, drawn by the Author.   Price 5*l.* 15*s.* 6*d.* cloth.

EACH VOLUME MAY BE HAD SEPARATELY.
Vol. I. The FOUNDATIONS, with 21 Plates. Price 2*l.* 2*s.* 2nd Edition.
Vol. II. THE SEA STORIES, with 20 Plates. Price 2*l.* 2*s.*
Vol. III. THE FALL, with 12 Plates. Price 1*l.* 11*s.* 6*d.*

The Seven Lamps of Architecture.

Second Edition, with Fourteen Plates drawn by the Author. Imp. 8vo. Price 1*l.* 1*s.* cloth.

Lectures on Architecture and Painting.

With Fourteen Cuts, drawn by the Author. Second Edition, crown 8vo. Price 8*s.* 6*d.* cloth.

Selections from the Writings of J. Ruskin, M.A.

One Volume. Post 8vo, with a Portrait. Price 6*s.* cloth.

"Unto this Last."

Four Essays on the First Principles of Political Economy.
With Preface. Fcap 8vo. 3*s.* 6*d.* cloth.

Pre-Raphaelitism.

A New Edition. Demy 8vo. Price 2*s.*

The Two Paths:

Being Lectures on Art, and its relation to Manufactures and Decoration.
One vol., crown 8vo, with Two Steel Engravings.   Price 7*s.* 6*d.* cloth.

The Elements of Drawing

Sixth Thousand, crown 8vo, with Illustrations drawn by the Author. Price 7*s.* 6*d.* cloth.

The Elements of Perspective.

With 80 Diagrams, crown 8vo. Price 3*s.* 6*d.* cloth.

The Political Economy of Art.

Price 2*s.* 6*d.* cloth.

RELIGIOUS.

Sermons:
By the late Rev. Fred. W. Robertson,
Incumbent of Trinity Chapel, Brighton.
FIRST SERIES.— Ninth Edition, post
8vo. Price 9s. cloth.
SECOND SERIES. — Eighth Edition.
Price 9s. cloth.
THIRD SERIES.—Seventh Edition, post
8vo, with Portrait. Price 9s. cloth.

Expositions of St. Paul's Epistles to the Corinthians.
By the late Rev. Fred. W. Robertson.
Second Edition. One thick Volume,
post 8vo. Price 10s. 6d. cloth.

Lectures and Addresses.
By the late Fredk. W. Robertson,
A New Edition. Fcap 8vo. 5s. cloth.

The Gospel in the Miracles of Christ.
By Rev. Richd. Travers Smith, M.A.
Chaplain of St. Stephen's, Dublin.
Fcap 8vo, price 5s. cloth.

Sermons:
Preached at Lincoln's Inn Chapel.
By the Rev. F. D. Maurice, M.A.
FIRST SERIES, 2 vols., post 8vo, price
21s. cloth.
SECOND SERIES, 2 vols., post 8vo,
price 21s. cloth.
THIRD SERIES, 2 vols., post 8vo,
price 21s. cloth.

Experiences of an English Sister of Mercy.
By Margaret Goodman.
3rd edit. revised, Fcap 8vo. 3s. 6d. cloth.

Tauler's Life and Sermons.
Translated by Miss Susanna Winkworth.
With Preface by Rev. C. KINGSLEY.
Small 4to, price 7s. 6d. cloth.

The Soul's Exodus and Pilgrimage.
By the Rev. J. Baldwin Brown,
Author of "The Divine Life in Man."
Second Edition. Crown 8vo.
Price 7s. 6d. cloth.

"Is it not Written?"
Being the Testimony of Scripture
against the Errors of Romanism.
By Edward S. Pryce, A.B.
Post 8vo. Price 6s. cloth.

Quakerism, Past and Present:
Being an Inquiry into the Causes of
its Decline.
By John S. Rowntree.
Post 8vo. Price 5s. cloth.
*** This Essay gained the First Prize
of One Hundred Guineas offered for
the best Essay on the subject.

The Peculium;
An Essay on the Causes of the Decline
of the Society of Friends.
By Thomas Hancock,
Post 8vo. Price 5s. cloth.
*** This Essay gained the Second
Prize of Fifty Guineas, which was
afterwards increased to One Hundred.

THE BISHOP OF SALISBURY v. DR. WILLIAMS.
The Defence of Dr. Rowland Williams;
Being a Report of the Speech delivered
in the Court of Arches, by JAMES
FITZJAMES STEPHEN, M.A., Recorder
of Newark-on-Trent. Published
from the Shorthand Writer's Notes,
Revised and Corrected. Post 8vo.
Price 10s. 6d. cloth.

MISCELLANEOUS.

The Correspondence of Leigh Hunt.
Edited by his Eldest Son.
Two Vols. Post 8vo, with Portrait. Price 24s. cloth.

The Port and Trade of London:
Historical, Statistical, Local, and General.
By Charles Capper,
Manager of the Victoria (London) Docks. Price 15s. cloth. 8vo.

New Zealand and the War.
By William Swainson, Esq.
Author of "New Zealand and its Colozation." Post 8vo. 5s. cloth.

The Lady's Guide to the Ordering of Her Household, and the Economy of the Dinner Table.
By a Lady.
Crown 8vo. Price 10s. 6d. cloth.

The Early Italian Poets.
Translated by D. G. Rossetti.
Part I.—Poets chiefly before Dante. Part II. — Dante and his Circle. Price 12s. cloth. Post 8vo.

The Book of Good Counsels:
Being an Abridged Translation of the Sanscrit Classic, the "Hitopadesa."
By Edwin Arnold, M.A., Oxon.
Author of "Education in India," &c. With Illustrations by Harrison Weir. Crown 8vo, 5s. cloth.

Education in Oxford:
Its Method, its Aids, and its Rewards.
By James E. Thorold Rogers, M.A.
Post 8vo, price 6s. cloth.

Household Education.
By Harriet Martineau.
A New Edition. Post 8vo. Price 5s. cloth.

Ragged London.
By John Hollingshead.
Post 8vo, 7s. 6d. cloth.

Household Medicine; and Sick-room Guide.
Describing Diseases, their Nature, Causes, and Symptoms, with the most approved Methods of Treatment, and the Properties and Uses of many new Remedies.
By John Gardner, M.D.
8vo, with numerous Illustrations. Price 10s. 6d. cloth.

The Four Georges:
Sketches of Manners, Morals, Court and Town Life.
By W. M. Thackeray.
With Illustrations. Crown 8vo. Price 5s. cloth.

Shakspere and his Birthplace.
By John R. Wise.
With 22 Illustrations by W. J. Linton. Crown 8vo. Printed on Toned Paper, and handsomely bound in ornamental cloth, gilt edges, price 7s. 6d.
. Also a cheap edition, 2s. 6d. cloth.

Man and his Dwelling Place.

An Essay towards the Interpretation of Nature.

Second Edition. With a New Preface. Crown 8vo, 6s. cloth.

———◆◇◆———

The Conduct of Life.

By Ralph Waldo Emerson,

Author of "Essays," "Representative Men," &c. Post 8vo, price 6s. cloth.
. Also a Cheap Edition, 1s. cloth.

———◆◇◆———

Social Innovators and their Schemes.

By William Lucas Sargant.
Post 8vo. Price 10s. 6d. cloth.

———◆◇◆———

Ethica;

Or, Characteristics of Men, Manners, and Books.
By Arthur Lloyd Windsor.
Demy 8vo. Price 12s. cloth.

———◆◇◆———

Bermuda:

Its History, Geology, Climate, Products, Agriculture, &c. &c.

By Theodore L. Godet, M.D.
Post 8vo, price 9s. cloth.

———◆◇◆———

Annals of British Legislation:

A Classified Summary of Parliamentary Papers.
Edited by Dr. Leone Levi.
The yearly issue consists of 1,000 pages, super-royal 8vo, and the Subscription is Two Guineas, payable in advance. Vols. I. to X. may now be had. Price 10l. 10s. cloth.

A Handbook of Average.

With a Chapter on Arbitration.
By Manley Hopkins.
Second Edition, Revised and brought down to the present time.
8vo. Price 15s. cloth; 17s. 6d. half-bound law calf.

———◆◇◆———

Sea Officer's Manual.

Being a Compendium of the Duties of Commander and Officers in the Mercantile Navy.
By Captain Alfred Parish.
Second Edition. Small post 8vo. Price 5s. cloth.

———◆◇◆———

Manual of the Mercantile Law

Of Great Britain and Ireland.
By Dr. Leone Levi.
8vo. Price 12s. cloth.

———◆◇◆———

Commercial Law of the World.

By Dr. Leone Levi.
Two vols. royal 4to. Price 6l. cloth.

———◆◇◆———

Victoria,

Or the Australian Gold Mines in 1857.
By William Westgarth.
Post 8vo, with Maps. 10s. 6d. cloth.

———◆◇◆———

New Zealand and its Colonization.

By William Swainson, Esq.
Demy 8vo. Price 14s. cloth.

The Education of the Human Race.

Now first Translated from the German of Lessing.

Fcap. 8vo, antique cloth. Price 4s.

Life in Spain.

By Walter Thornbury.

Two Vols. post 8vo, with Eight Tinted Illustrations, price 21s.

A Treatise on Rifles, Cannon, and Sporting Arms.

Gunnery :

By William Greener,

Author of "The Gun."
Demy 8vo, with Illustrations.
Price 14s. cloth.

On the Strength of Nations.

By Andrew Bisset, M.A.

Post 8vo. Price 9s. cloth.

Results of Astronomical Observations

Made at the Cape of Good Hope.

By Sir John Herschel.

4to, with Plates. Price 4l. 4s. cloth.

Astronomical Observations.

Made at the Sydney Observatory in the year 1859.

By W. Scott, M.A.

8vo. 6s.

On the Treatment of the Insane,

Without Mechanical Restraints,
By John Conolly, M.D.

Demy 8vo. Price 14s. cloth.

England and her Soldiers.

By Harriet Martineau.

With Three Plates of Illustrative Diagrams. 1 vol. crown 8vo, price 9s. cloth.

Grammar and Dictionary of the Malay Language.

By John Crawfurd, Esq.

Two vols. 8vo. Price 36s. cloth.

Tea Planting in the Himalaya.

By A. T. McGowan.

8vo, with Frontispiece, price 5s. cloth.

Signs of the Times ;

Or, The Dangers to Religious Liberty in the Present Day.

By Chevalier Bunsen.

Translated by Miss S. WINKWORTH.
One vol. 8vo. Price 5s. cloth.

Wit and Humour.

By Leigh Hunt.

Price 5s. cloth.

Jar of Honey from Hybla.

By Leigh Hunt.

Price 5s. cloth.

Men, Women, and Books.
By Leigh Hunt.
Two vols. Price 10s. cloth.

Zoology of South Africa.
By Dr. Andrew Smith.
Royal 4to, cloth, with Coloured Plates.

MAMMALIA	£2
AVES	7
REPTILIA	5
PISCES	2
INVERTEBRATA	1

Religion in Common Life.
By William Ellis.
Post 8vo. Price 7s. 6d. cloth.

Life of Sir Robert Peel.
By Thomas Doubleday.
Two vols. 8vo. Price 18s. cloth.

Principles of Agriculture;
Especially Tropical.
By B. Lovell Phillips, M.D.
Demy 8vo. Price 7s. 6d. cloth.

Books for the Blind.
Printed in raised Roman letters, at
the Glasgow Asylum.

SMITH, ELDER AND CO.'S SHILLING SERIES

OF

STANDARD WORKS OF FICTION.

Well printed, on good paper, and tastefully bound.

Price ONE SHILLING each Volume,

SECOND ISSUE.

LOST AND WON. By Georgiana M. Craik.
HAWKSVIEW. By Holme Lee.
FLORENCE TEMPLAR. By Mrs. F. Vidal.

COUSIN STELLA; OR, CONFLICT. By the Author of "Who Breaks—Pays."
HIGHLAND LASSIES; OR, THE ROUA PASS.

FIRST ISSUE.

CONFIDENCES. By the author of "Rita."
ERLESMERE; OR, CONTRASTS OF CHARACTER. By L. S. Lavenu.
NANETTE AND HER LOVERS. By Talbot Gwynne.
THE LIFE AND DEATH OF SILAS BARNSTARKE. By Talbot Gwynne.
TENDER AND TRUE. By the Author of "Claran."

ROSE DOUGLAS; the Autobiography of a Scotch Minister's Daughter.
GILBERT MASSENGER. By Holme Lee.
MY LADY: A Tale of Modern Life.
THORNEY HALL: A Story of an Old Family. By Holme Lee.
THE CRUELEST WRONG OF ALL.

WORKS ON INDIA AND THE EAST.

The Wild Sports of India,
With detailed Instructions for the Sportsman; to which are added Remarks on the Breeding and Rearing of Horses, and the Formation of Light Irregular Cavalry
By Major Henry Shakespear,
late Commandant Nagpore Irregular Force. With Portrait of the Author. Second Edition, much Enlarged. Post 8vo. Price 10s. cloth.

Cotton; an Account of its Culture in the Bombay Presidency.
By Walter Cassels.
8vo, price 16s. cloth.

Narrative of the North China Campaign of 1860.
By Robert Swinhoe.
Staff Interpreter to Sir Hope Grant. 8vo, with Illustrations. 12s. cloth.

A Visit to the Suez Canal Works.
By George Percy Badger.
Demy 8vo. With Map. Price 2s. 6d.

PRIZE ESSAY.
Caste:
Considered under its Moral, Social, and Religious Aspects.
By Arthur J. Patterson, B.A., of Trinity College.
Post 8vo. Price 4s. 6d. cloth.

The Sanitary Condition of Indian Jails.
By Joseph Ewart, M.D.,
Bengal Medical Service.
With Plans, 8vo. Price 16s. cloth.

Egypt, Nubia, and Ethiopia.
Illustrated by 100 Stereoscopic Photographs, taken by Francis Frith, for Messrs. Negretti and Zambra; with Descriptions and numerous Wood Engravings, by Joseph Bonomi, F.R.S.L., and Notes by Samuel Sharpe. In One Vol. small 4to. Elegantly bound. Price 3l. 3s.

Campaigning Experiences
In Rajpootana and Central India during the Mutiny in 1857–8.
By Mrs. Henry Duberly.
Post 8vo, with Map. Price 10s. 6d. cloth.

Narrative of the Mutinies in Oude.
By Captain G. Hutchinson,
Military Secretary, Oude.
Post 8vo. Price 10s. cloth.

A Lady's Escape from Gwalior
During the Mutinies of 1857.
By Mrs. Coopland.
Post 8vo. Price 10s. 6d.

Views and Opinions of Gen. Jacob, C.B.
Edited by Captain Lewis Pelly.
Demy 8vo. Price 12s. cloth.

Papers of the late Lord Metcalfe.
By John William Kaye.
Demy 8vo. Price 16s. cloth.

The English in India.
By Philip Anderson, A.M.
Second Edition, 8vo. Price 14s. cloth.

Indian Exchange Tables.

By J. H. Roberts.

8vo. Second Edition, enlarged.
Price 10s. 6d. cloth.

Christianity in India.

A Historical Narrative.

By John William Kaye.

8vo. Price 16s. cloth.

The Parsees :

Their History, Religion, Manners, and
Customs.

By Dosabhoy Framjee.

Post 8vo. Price 10s. cloth.

The Vital Statistics

Of the European and Native Armies
in India.

By Joseph Ewart, M.D.

Demy 8vo. Price 9s. cloth.

The Bhilsa Topes ;

Or, Buddhist Monuments of Central
India.

By Major Cunningham.

One vol. 8vo, with Thirty-three Plates.
Price 30s. cloth.

The Chinese and their Rebellions.

By Thomas Taylor Meadows.

One thick volume, 8vo, with Maps.
Price 18s. cloth.

Hong Kong to Manilla.

By Henry T. Ellis, R.N.

Post 8vo, with Fourteen Illustrations.
Price 12s. cloth.

The Botany of the Himalaya.

By Dr. Forbes Royle.

Two vols. roy. 4to, cloth, with Coloured
Plates. Reduced to 5l. 5s.

The Defence of Lucknow.

By Captain Thomas F. Wilson.

Sixth Thousand. With Plan. Small
post 8vo. Price 2s. 6d.

PRIZE ESSAYS.

By B. A. Irving.

The Theory of Caste,

8vo. 5s. cloth.

The Commerce of India with Europe.

Post 8vo. Price 7s. 6d. cloth.

Moohummudan Law of Sale.

By N. B. E. Baillie, Esq.

8vo. Price 14s. cloth.

Moohummudan Law of Inheritance.

By N. B. E. Baillie, Esq.

8vo. Price 8s. cloth.

The Cauvery, Kistnah, and Godavery :

Being a Report on the Works con-
structed on those Rivers, for the
Irrigation of Provinces in the Pre-
sidency of Madras.

By Col. R. Baird Smith, F.G.S.

Demy 8vo, with 19 Plans. 28s. cloth.

Land Tax of India.

According to the Moohummudan Law.

By N. B. E. Baillie, Esq.

8vo. Price 6s. cloth.

FICTION.

A Loss Gained.
By Philip Cresswell.
In One Volume.

Carr of Carrlyon.
By Hamilton Aïdé.
Author of "Rita," &c. 3 vols.

The Cotton Lord.
By Herbert Glyn.
Two Vols.

Warp and Woof.
By Holme Lee.
Three Vols.

Said and Done.
In One Vol.

Who Breaks—Pays.
In Two Vols.
By the Author of " Cousin Stella."

The Wortlebank Diary :
With Stories from Kathie Brande's
Portfolio.
By Holme Lee. Three Vols.

Over the Cliffs.
By Mrs. Chanter,
Author of " Ferny Combes." 2 vols.

Lovel the Widower.
By W. M. Thackeray.
With six Illustrations. Post 8vo.
Price 6s. cloth.

Esmond.
By W. M. Thackeray.
Third Edition, crown 8vo. Price 6s.
cloth.

Scarsdale ;
Or, Life on the Lancashire and York-
shire Border Thirty Years ago. 3 vols.

Agnes of Sorrento.
By Mrs. Harriet Beecher Stowe.
Post 8vo. Price 7s. 6d. cloth.

Herbert Chauncey :
A Man more Sinned against than
Sinning.
By Sir Arthur Hallam Elton, Bart.
In 3 vols.

Hills and Plains.
Two Vols.

The Firstborn.
By the Author of " My Lady."
Three volumes.

The Tragedy of Life.
By John H. Brenten. Two Vols.

Framley Parsonage.
By Anthony Trollope,
Illustrated by J. E. Millais, R.A.
Three Vols. Post 8vo, 21s. cloth.
Also a cheap Edition. 1 vol., post 8vo
Price 5s. cloth.

Phantastes :
A Faerie Romance for Men and
Women.
By George Macdonald.
Post 8vo. Price 10s. 6d. cloth.

The Fool of Quality.
By Henry Brooke.
New and Revised Edition, with Biogra-
phical Preface by the Rev. CHAS.
KINGSLEY, Rector of Eversley.
Two vols., post 8vo, with Portrait of
the Author, price 21s.

CHEAP EDITIONS OF POPULAR WORKS.

Lavinia.
Price 2*s.* 6*d.* cloth.

Sylvan Holt's Daughter.
By Holme Lee.
Price 2*s.* 6*d.* cloth.

The Autobiography of Leigh Hunt.
Price 2*s.* 6*d.* cloth.

WORKS OF THE BRONTE SISTERS.
Price 2*s.* 6*d.* each vol.
By Currer Bell.

The Professor.
To which are added the POEMS of Currer, Ellis, and Acton Bell. Now first collected.

Jane Eyre.
Shirley.
Villette.

Wuthering Heights and Agnes Grey.
By Ellis and Acton Bell.
With Memoir by CURRER BELL.

The Tenant of Wildfell Hall.
By Acton Bell.

Life of Charlotte Brontë
(Currer Bell).
By Mrs. Gaskell.
Cheap edition. 2*s.* 6*d.* cloth.

Lectures on the English Humourists
Of the Eighteenth Century.
By W. M. Thackeray.
Price 2*s.* 6*d.* cloth.

The Town.
By Leigh Hunt.
With Forty-five Engravings.
Price 2*s.* 6*d.* cloth.

Transformation.
By Nathaniel Hawthorne.
Price 2*s.* 6*d.* cloth.

Kathie Brande:
The Fireside History of a Quiet Life.
By Holme Lee.   Price 2*s.* 6*d.* cloth.

Below the Surface.
By Sir A. H. Elton, Bart., M.P.
Price 2*s.* 6*d.* cloth.

British India.
By Harriet Martineau. 2*s.* 6*d.* cloth.

Italian Campaigns of General Bonaparte.
By George Hooper.
With a Map.   Price 2*s.* 6*d.* cloth.

Deerbrook.
By Harriet Martineau.   2*s.* 6*d.* cloth.

Tales of the Colonies.
By Charles Rowcroft. 2*s.* 6*d.* cloth.

A Lost Love.
By Ashford Owen. 2*s.* cloth.

Romantic Tales
(Including "Avillion").
By the Author of "John Halifax, Gentleman." 2*s.* 6*d.* cloth.

Domestic Stories.
By the same Author. 2*s.* 6*d.* cloth.

After Dark.
By Wilkie Collins. 2*s.* 6*d.* cloth.

School for Fathers.
By Talbot Gwynne. 2*s.* cloth.

Paul Ferroll.
Price 2*s.* cloth.

JUVENILE AND EDUCATIONAL.

The Parents' Cabinet
Of Amusement and Instruction for Young Persons.
New Edition, revised, in Twelve Shilling Volumes, with numerous Illustrations.

*** The work is now complete in 4 vols. extra cloth, gilt edges, at 3s. 6d. each; or in 6 vols. extra cloth, gilt edges, at 2s. 6d. each.
Every volume is complete in itself, and sold separately.

By the Author of "Round the Fire," &c.

Round the Fire :
Six Stories for Young Readers.
Square 16mo, with Four Illustrations. Price 2s. 6d. cloth.

Unica :
A Story for a Sunday Afternoon.
With Four Illustrations. 2s. 6d. cloth.

Old Gingerbread and the Schoolboys.
With Four Coloured Plates. 2s. 6d. cl.

Willie's Birthday :
Showing how a Little Boy did what he Liked, and how he Enjoyed it.
With Four Illustrations. 2s. cloth.

Willie's Rest :
A Sunday Story.
With Four Illustrations. 2s. cloth.

Uncle Jack, the Fault Killer.
With Four Illustrations. 2s. 6d. cloth.

Philo-Socrates.
Parts I. & II. "Among the Boys."
Part III., IV.—"Among the Teachers."
By William Ellis.
Post 8vo. Price 1s. each.

Legends from Fairy Land.
By Holme Lee,
Author of "Kathie Brande," "Sylvan Holt's Daughter," &c.
With Eight Illustrations. 3s. 6d. cloth.

The Wonderful Adventures of Tuflongbo and his Elfin Company in their Journey with Little Content, through the Enchanted Forest.
By Holme Lee,
Author of "Legends from Fairy Land," &c.
With Eight Illustrations. Fcap 8vo. Price 3s. 6d. cloth.

The King of the Golden River ;
Or, the Black Brothers.
By John Ruskin, M.A.
Third Edition, with 22 Illustrations by Richard Doyle. Price 2s. 6d.

Elementary Works on Social Economy.
By William Ellis.
Uniform in foolscap 8vo, half-bound.
I.—OUTLINES OF SOCIAL ECONOMY. 1s. 6d.
II.—PROGRESSIVE LESSONS IN SOCIAL SCIENCE.
III.—INTRODUCTION TO THE SOCIAL SCIENCES. 2s.
IV.—OUTLINES OF THE UNDERSTANDING. 2s.
V.—WHAT AM I? WHERE AM I? WHAT OUGHT I TO DO? &c. 1s. sewed.

Rhymes for Little Ones.
16 Illustrations. 1s. 6d. cl., gilt edges.

Stories from the Parlour Printing Press.
By the Authors of the "Parent's Cabinet."
Fcap 8vo. Price 2s. cloth.

Juvenile Miscellany.
Six Engravings. Price 2s. 6d. cloth.

RECENT POETRY.

Cache-Cache.
By William Davy Watson, M.A.
Fcap 8vo. Price 4s. cloth.

Poems.
By the Rev. George E. Maunsell.
Fcap 8vo. Price 5s. cloth.

Christ's Company, and other Poems.
By Richard Watson Dixon, M.A.
Fcap 8vo, price 5s. cloth.

Sybil, and other Poems.
By John Lyttelton.
Fcap 8vo, price 4s. cloth.

Stories in Verse for the Street and Lane:
By Mrs. Sewell.
3rd Thousand. Post 8vo. Cloth, 1s.

Edwin and Ethelburga:
A Drama.
By Frederick W. Wyon.
Fcap 8vo. Price 4s. cloth.

A Man's Heart: a Poem.
By Dr. Charles Mackay.
Post 8vo. Price 5s. cloth.

Hannibal; a Drama.
Fcap 8vo. Price 5s. cloth.

Shelley; and other Poems.
By John Alfred Langford.
Fcap 8vo. Price 5s. cloth.

Isabel Gray; or, The Mistress Didn't Know.
By Mrs. Sewell,
Post 8vo. Cloth. Gilt edges. 1s.

Homely Ballads
For the Working Man's Fireside.
By Mary Sewell.
13th Thousand. Post 8vo. Cloth, 1s.

Memories of Merton.
By John Bruce Norton.
Fcap 8vo. Price 5s. cloth.

THE CORNHILL MAGAZINE:
Price One Shilling Monthly, with Illustrations.

VOLUMES I., II., III., IV., and V., each containing 768 pages of Letterpress, with 12 Illustrations, and numerous Vignettes and Diagrams, are published, handsomely bound in Embossed Cloth. Price 7s. 6d. each.

For the convenience of Subscribers, the Embossed CLOTH COVERS for each Volume are sold separately, price One Shilling.

READING COVERS for separate Numbers have also been prepared, price Sixpence in plain Cloth, or One Shilling and Sixpence in French Morocco.

London: Printed by SMITH, ELDER and Co., Little Green Arbour Court, Old Bailey, E.C.

2071 C07

Trieste

Trieste Publishing has a massive catalogue of classic book titles. Our aim is to provide readers with the highest quality reproductions of fiction and non-fiction literature that has stood the test of time. The many thousands of books in our collection have been sourced from libraries and private collections around the world.

The titles that Trieste Publishing has chosen to be part of the collection have been scanned to simulate the original. Our readers see the books the same way that their first readers did decades or a hundred or more years ago. Books from that period are often spoiled by imperfections that did not exist in the original. Imperfections could be in the form of blurred text, photographs, or missing pages. It is highly unlikely that this would occur with one of our books. Our extensive quality control ensures that the readers of Trieste Publishing's books will be delighted with their purchase. Our staff has thoroughly reviewed every page of all the books in the collection, repairing, or if necessary, rejecting titles that are not of the highest quality. This process ensures that the reader of one of Trieste Publishing's titles receives a volume that faithfully reproduces the original, and to the maximum degree possible, gives them the experience of owning the original work.

We pride ourselves on not only creating a pathway to an extensive reservoir of books of the finest quality, but also providing value to every one of our readers. Generally, Trieste books are purchased singly - on demand, however they may also be purchased in bulk. Readers interested in bulk purchases are invited to contact us directly to enquire about our tailored bulk rates. Email: customerservice@triestepublishing.com

You May Also Like

ISBN: 9780649619146
Paperback: 140 pages
Dimensions: 6.14 x 0.30 x 9.21 inches
Language: eng

Joseph Guy's School Expositor; Or, the Learner's New Spelling Assistant

Joseph Guy, Jun.

ISBN: 9780649691807
Paperback: 244 pages
Dimensions: 6.14 x 0.51 x 9.21 inches
Language: eng

Geological Survey of Missouri: A Preliminary Report on the Coal Deposits of Missouri from Field Work Prosecuted During the Years 1890 and 1891

Arthur Winslow

www.triestepublishing.com

You May Also Like

ISBN: 9780649573073
Paperback: 146 pages
Dimensions: 6.14 x 0.31 x 9.21 inches
Language: eng

ELva's Revenge, a Legend Poem, in Five Cantos. With Other Poems

F. W. J. Morris

ISBN: 9780649731213
Paperback: 160 pages
Dimensions: 6.14 x 0.34 x 9.21 inches
Language: eng

War Poems, 1898

California Club & Irving M. Scott

www.triestepublishing.com

You May Also Like

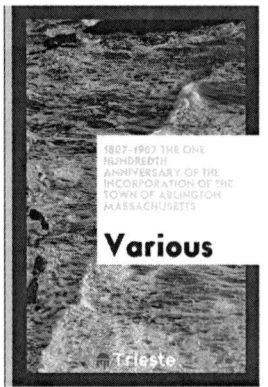

ISBN: 9780649420544
Paperback: 108 pages
Dimensions: 6.14 x 0.22 x 9.21 inches
Language: eng

1807-1907 The One Hundredth Anniversary of the incorporation of the Town of Arlington Massachusetts

Various

ISBN: 9780649194292
Paperback: 44 pages
Dimensions: 6.14 x 0.09 x 9.21 inches
Language: eng

Biennial report of the Board of State Harbor Commissioners, for the two fiscal years commencing July 1, 1890, and ending June 30, 1892

Various

You May Also Like

ISBN: 9780649199693
Paperback: 48 pages
Dimensions: 6.14 x 0.10 x 9.21 inches
Language: eng

Biennial report of the Board of State Harbor Commissioners for the two fisca years. Commeneing July 1, 1884, and Ending June 30, 1886

Various

ISBN: 9780649196395
Paperback: 44 pages
Dimensions: 6.14 x 0.09 x 9.21 inches
Language: eng

Biennial report of the Board of state commissioners, for the two fiscal years, commencing July 1, 1890, and ending June 30, 1892

Various

Find more of our titles on our website. We have a selection of thousands of titles that will interest you. Please visit

www.triestepublishing.com

CPSIA information can be obtained
at www.ICGtesting.com
Printed in the USA
LVOW07s0957131017
552308LV00003B/17/P

9 780649 694563